**Program Directors as Staff Trainers**: contains such practical aids as a Director's Self-Evaluation Checklist…7 activities that help pinpoint areas for needs assessment and training…a checklist to measure stress levels among staff…and 8 ways administrators can prevent their own stress or burnout while balancing their multiple roles.

**Using Outside Directors to Meet Staff Development Needs**: discusses how to judge whether use of a consultant is necessary…how to identify and select a consultant…how to determine what amount is necessary for consultant fees…and how to choose a college course as a staff development option.

**A Program Model and Techniques for Performance-Based Assessment**: explains some of the programs you can use to facilitate and assess teacher skills, particularly the Child Development Associate Credential Award system.

**Training Parents and Other Volunteer Staff**: contains aids for orienting, training, and evaluating parents, senior citizens, community organizations, and student teachers–including a Parent Involvement Questionnaire and a sample agenda for a volunteer orientation workshop.

**Funding Sources and Other Techniques for Providing Staff Development**: provides helpful hints for pursuing federal funding, foundation grants, center-based volunteer efforts, and such innovative approaches as service exchange programs, inservice education alternatives, and community resources.

**Evaluating Staff Development Programs**: includes standard and specially designed tools for examining the impact of staff development and training on individuals and the environment of early childhood programs.

**Resources for Staff Development and Training**: lists the range of professional organizations, journals, and materials available to assist preschool administrators.

Also included throughout are 32 sample charts, checklists, and forms that you can use to accomplish specific tasks–each ready to be copied as it is or adapted to fit the particular needs.

# PRESCHOOL DIRECTOR'S STAFF DEVELOPMENT HANDBOOK

Kathleen Pullan Watkins, Ed.D.
Lucius Durant, Jr., M.Ed.

The Center for Applied Research in Education
West Nyack, New York

**Library of Congress Cataloging-in-Publication Data**

Watkins, Kathleen Pullan.
    Preschool director's staff development handbook.

    Includes bibliographies and index.
    1. Education, Preschool—Personnel management—
Handbooks, manuals, etc.   2. Preschool teachers—
In-service training—Handbooks, manuals, etc.
3. Career development—Handbooks, manuals, etc.
I. Durant, Lucius, 1932–    . II. Title.
LB1140.27.W37  1987     372.11'46     87-13220

ISBN 0-87628-107-2

THE CENTER FOR APPLIED
RESEARCH IN EDUCATION
A division of Simon & Schuster
West Nyack, N.Y.

Printed in the United States of America

# ABOUT THIS HANDBOOK

FOR EARLY CHILDHOOD practitioners, developing a professional identity is one of our major concerns. It has taken many years to promote acceptance of the importance of the earliest years of life and the contributions that may be made to young children's development by high-quality programs.

Despite these advances in attitude, there is still the tendency to devalue the roles of day-care providers, child-care workers, and early childhood educators— a tendency to equate the professional responsibilities of these persons with the functions of parenting.

It has become increasingly important for administrators, directors, head teachers, and everyone who manages young children's programs to provide activities for promoting the professional growth of staff, while insuring the quality of the overall program. Beside the desire for recognition, early childhood educators have additional reasons for an emphasis on staff development.

- Parents are increasingly aware of the importance of early education and often ask teachers and caregivers about developmental and curricular issues for which answers are both expected and needed.

- A growing awareness of stress and burnout contributes to the urgent need for staff development. Research shows that human services personnel are less likely to suffer stress if professional support, developmental stimulus, and a sense of job satisfaction are provided.

- Another impetus for strong staff development is standards that permit many early childhood centers to hire entry-level workers with a wide variety of educational and experiential backgrounds. Many of these individuals rely on their early childhood programs to provide opportunities for professional development and career advancement. A sensitive leader with a well-thought-out staff development program offers such possibilities through inservice, outside training programs, and a variety of staff-development activities.

We acknowledge that many conscientious early childhood administrators are working to provide quality programming for young children. We salute the great numbers of directors, program supervisors, and head teachers who demonstrate their belief that effective programming is often founded in a strong, unified staff. It is for just such persons that *Preschool Director's Staff Development Handbook* is written, as many administrators need support systems and basic guidelines to accomplish staff development goals. To help all administrators achieve these ends, this book contains the following special features:

- Activities for planning, implementing, and evaluating staff development
- Techniques for identifying staff development needs
- Samples of many useful forms
- Methods for developing training programs
- Tips to assist the director as staff trainer
- Innovative training models
- Sample programs that use staff-development activities to promote change
- Suggestions for orienting and training volunteer workers
- Techniques for identifying and working with consultants
- Methods for identifying many types of available staff development resources

Administrators can use *Preschool Director's Staff Development Handbook* in several ways. Since each chapter covers a different staff development topic, the Table of Contents may be used as a reference to locate assistance for many specific program-development or problem areas. For example, if an outside consultant has been selected to provide staff training on a particular topic, Chapter 7, "Using Outside Consultants to Meet Staff Development Needs," can be helpful in the process of scheduling, preparing your staff for training activities, evaluating, and following up training events.

Although all the chapters may be used independently, we hope you will find that the book also represents a comprehensive overview of the entire staff development process. The many forms and examples will enable even the busiest administrators to provide appropriate, successful staff development to meet the needs of their particular programs.

It is our strong belief that the highest quality early childhood programs are built with persons who understand both theory and practice, are open to change, and are willing to be exposed frequently to new ideas and challenging situations. These are the true professionals who continually grow, change, and develop.

*Kathleen Pullan Watkins*

*Lucius Durant, Jr.*

# TABLE OF CONTENTS

# The Need for Staff Development in Early Childhood Programs

DEVELOPING QUALITY early childhood programs is one of the great social and educational challenges of the 1980s. Today's nursery schools, day-care centers, play groups, and primary school programs play a vital part in the overall development of many young children. A great deal of a youngster's critical physical, social, and cognitive growth takes place in the first five years of life, and much is completed by age nine.

The impact of these programs is not limited to their effect on participating children however; also affected are the parents, siblings and extended families of those youngsters who receive early childhood services. These schools and centers* do not merely provide learning experiences for small children; they are also gathering and learning sites for the entire family. Many mothers and fathers rely on their child's teacher to provide child development information, advice regarding child-rearing problems, and the reassurance and support that young families often require to cope during their youngsters' early years.

With such potential for impact on the family and community, the roles of the individual members of an early childhood staff have taken on unexpected dimensions. Once considered babysitters, today's teacher/caregiver* is expected to be a high-level professional. The many responsibilities of the administrator-directors* of these programs are now complicated by the tasks of developing program components and preparing staff to address goals that involve children, parents, and community, a task that too few early childhood administrators are trained to assume. Thus, providing guidelines and resources for those responsible for staff development and training is the focus of this book.

## DEFINITIONS OF *STAFF DEVELOPMENT* AND *TRAINING*

By way of clarification, *staff development* refers to one component of an early childhood program, a segment designed to promote the professional growth of individual staff members as well as that of the staff unit. *Training,* another term that will appear frequently in this volume, refers to one of the many facets of staff development, one in which staff are participants in sessions

---

*Although early childhood programs and their administrators are referred to in various ways across the country, the term *center* will be used in this book to denote a program and *director* will be used when the program's administrator is discussed. *Caregiver* will often be used in reference to a person providing direct service to children.

or seminars aimed at providing them with specific skills or knowledge. The program's director assumes responsibility for personnel in both of these important areas, although directors are not always those who conduct training.

## DESIGNING A STAFF DEVELOPMENT COMPONENT

John Goodlad[1] suggests that school personnel often expect children to be eagerly receptive to learning when their teachers' minds have grown stagnant. The most successful teachers, according to Goodlad, are those who are themselves actively involved in the growing and learning processes.

Staff development is a multifaceted component of the early childhood program. In its most concrete forms, it is a series of written plans describing professional goals set by and for each staff member, including those playing nonteaching roles. In its most complex and abstract form, it is an atmosphere that suggests to all that learning, sharing, and cooperation are valued as adult experiences, as much as they are desired for children.

The process of designing an effective staff development component begins with an administrator's study of program history in an effort to pinpoint the causes of past successes and failures. An examination of current needs is equally important to setting goals appropriate to the clients and the community being served. These steps are essential to the functioning of the program and critical to balancing program goals with staff skills. When the program's aims have been identified, the stage has been set for evaluating the ability of personnel to achieve these goals. Unfortunately, this process is often neglected, frequently resulting in the staff trying to address goals they have neither the experience, training, nor resources to accomplish (see Figure 1–1).

When the administrator discovers areas of weakness in staff ability or direction, these should be viewed as guideposts for designing the staff-development program. Inappropriate long-term goals should not be abandoned, but short-term objectives can be adjusted to reflect the staff's current qualifications. As new skills are developed through staff training and other professional growth activities, the aims of the early childhood program may be expanded.

Let's take a look at the following example of a staff development situation. The example involves the Grant Child Development Center, a fictitious program.

> The new director of the Grant Child Development Center would like to see all staff participating in weekly curriculum planning sessions. However, the previous Center administrator felt that this was the sole responsibility of the program's certified teachers. In order for inexperienced classroom assistants and aides to become involved in this activity, training will have to be provided in the development of lessons, activities, and the use of materials and equipment. Once accomplished,

## STEPS IN DESIGNING A STAFF DEVELOPMENT COMPONENT

5
Design a staff-
development
component to build
skills and maximize
strengths

4
Evaluate staff ability
to meet
programmatic aims

3
Develop appropriate
goals and objectives

2
Identify current
program needs

1
Study program
history to determine
causes of past
successes and failures

**FIGURE 1–1**

the training would enable the Center's personnel to be more involved in working toward one of the program goals for the year, "improving the quality and range of the children's daily program."

One of the many unique aspects of early childhood programs is that state-mandated staff-child ratios usually require child-care workers to work in small teams. Therefore, it is not enough to consider the development of the individual teacher, or even that of the staff as a whole. A director must also consider the functioning of those working in "partnership" fashion in each classroom. Each unit will have its own philosophy, codes of behavior, and styles of interaction. These are not behaviors or ideas created by the program's director. Instead, they are the result of the personalities and experiences of the staff in the unit. These situations can be strongly influenced by professional attitudes and demeanor of the Center's administrator, however, as well as by the training and other professional experiences provided.

## The Director's Plan

The director designing a staff development component studies the performance of personnel as they function singly and together, meets with individuals, teams, and the entire staff. These activities, observations, and discussions provide information useful for creating the staff development plans previously mentioned. A sample plan is shown in Figure 1–2.

Plans for staff development must be based on consultations with all of those who will be affected. The written plan should include indices of development in some or all of the following areas: staff training sessions; attendance at college classes, seminars, workshops, and conferences; reading professional journals, periodicals, and texts; and staff participation in center projects, such as parent-education programs, newsletters, and home-school events. Substitute staff or volunteers should be available to occasionally enable center personnel to be involved in out-of-school programs.

## The Nonteaching Support Staff's Role

One group of individuals who are often neglected in the staff development process are those who are members of the nonteaching support staff, including bus drivers, food service workers and clerical personnel. Persons responsible for meal preparation can learn about nutrition and nutrition education for young children, thus becoming curriculum-planning consultants and participants. Individuals who drive school buses may find it helpful to study aspects of child development and behavior management, for they spend a great deal of time transporting youngsters to and from school and often contend with many of the same situations faced by teachers. All staff can make significant contributions to their early childhood program, provided their talents and scope of their responsibilities are realized.

**STAFF DEVELOPMENT PLAN**

Center Name: Grant Child Development Center

Director: Rose Smith

School Year: 1987–88

Date of Plan Implementation: July 1, 1987

A. Personnel to be involved in staff development activities:

| Name | Position | Highest Level of Education Achieved/Field |
|------|----------|-------------------------------------------|
| Yvette M. | Head Teacher | Master's Degree/Early Childhood Education |
| Erica R. | Teacher | Bachelor's Degree/Child Development |
| Gayle L. | Teacher Assistant | Associate of Arts/Home Economics |
| Matthew D. | Teacher Assistant | Associate of Science/Biology |
| Alyson B. | Teacher Assistant | High School Diploma/College Preparatory |
| Jessica W. | Cook/Nutritionist | High School Diploma/Secretarial Science |

B. Program goals to be addressed by plan:

1. To offer an improved, expanded curriculum for children.
2. To facilitate more effective interactions among staff, children, and parents.
3. To develop an in-school environment more appropriate to the needs of children and staff.
4. To promote increased parent involvement in the school program.
5. To involve all staff in continuing education activities.

C. Suggested staff trainers/consultants:

| Name | Affiliation/Organization | Telephone |
|------|--------------------------|-----------|
| Mr. Ron Williams | Smith Preschool | 555-9876 |
| Dr. Gloria Jones | Penn State University | 555-1234 |

**FIGURE 1–2**

6

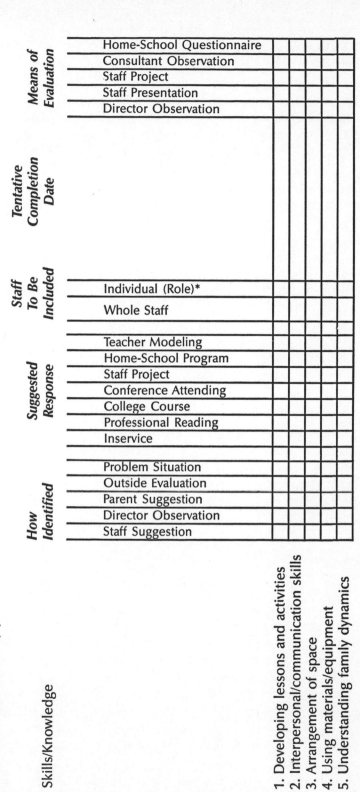

# STAFF DEVELOPMENT PLAN (Continued)

D. Community and other resources to be utilized:

University Bookstore, Teacher Center, Public Library, University Early Childhood Department, Early Childhood Directors' Support Group

E. Additional suggestions for improvement
—increase director observations and feedback to staff
—subscribe to early childhood journals and curriculum magazines

F. Skills to be addressed by plan:

Skills/Knowledge

| How Identified | Suggested Response | Staff To Be Included | Tentative Completion Date | Means of Evaluation |
|---|---|---|---|---|
| Problem Situation / Outside Evaluation / Parent Suggestion / Director Observation / Staff Suggestion | Teacher Modeling / Home-School Program / Staff Project / Conference Attending / College Course / Professional Reading / Inservice | Individual (Role)* / Whole Staff | | Home-School Questionnaire / Consultant Observation / Staff Project / Staff Presentation / Director Observation |

1. Developing lessons and activities
2. Interpersonal/communication skills
3. Arrangement of space
4. Using materials/equipment
5. Understanding family dynamics

*H.T. = head teacher; T = teacher; T-Assist = teacher assistant; T.A. = teacher aide; C.N. = cook/nutritionist

FIGURE 1–2 cont'd.

7

## The Center's Atmosphere

The atmosphere that promotes staff development activity is neither difficult to achieve nor intangible. It is, however, a tone generally set by those persons in leadership positions in an early childhood center. Encouragement is needed for individuals to share their own or accept another's professional interests. Administrative support can be the key to encouraging the shy person, or offsetting resentment or discomfort in another. An atmosphere conducive to staff development is indicated when the program director encourages the ideas and suggestions of parents and personnel, when the director maintains an eclectic approach and philosophy, and when the center's leader welcomes needed change rather than resisting it.

In such a center, there is a clear chain of command, and the words "open-door policy" have a familiar and meaningful sound. Staff with questions or problems feel free to discuss their concerns. Gossip and disagreements are avoided. This director has regular meetings and frequent informal contact with staff. All personnel are observed and receive feedback on their job performance at timely intervals. The director seeks and accepts comments from staff relative to the discharge of administrative duties.

Those who study stress and burnout in human service personnel, such as Barry Farber[2] of Teachers College, tell us that when these syndromes appear, one of the contributing factors is the feeling that one is unappreciated, unimportant in the scheme of things, and easily replaced. The administrator concerned about creating a positive atmosphere for staff development remains aware of the taxing nature of work with young children and recognizes each person's need for reinforcement. This director has a working knowledge of the phrases and gestures that say to staff, "I like what you are doing. Please, keep up the good work!"

## IDENTIFYING TRAINING NEEDS

Most plans for staff development include some indication of the need for training. Through research, pilot programs, and professional collaboration, new information is constantly becoming available to persons in the early childhood field. This information can assist teachers, child care workers, and support personnel in the provision of quality services. Furthermore, each new youngster entering a program presents a host of different challenges, problems, and questions. As a consequence, even certified teachers need refresher seminars dealing with child development topics, parenting issues, and related subjects.

Since there are a wide variety of possible topics for training, it is prudent for an early childhood administrator to spend some time observing and talking with staff members about their perception of training needs. Some personnel, familiar with self-evaluative techniques, are consistently and accurately aware of their strengths and weaknesses. Many others will require assistance to identify the training activities that will most benefit them.

When observing staff, a director should use predetermined criteria, rather than make subjective value judgments (see Chapter 8). This is especially appropriate when the administrator is a specialist trained in a field other than early childhood education. For example, when evaluating teacher performance, a checklist of teacher skills in the areas of daily planning, implementation of children's program, program evaluation, record keeping, and home-school relations would be helpful (see Chapter 8).

Many local and national early childhood organizations have lists of behavioral indicators or competencies appropriate for people working with young children.[3] Consulting these sources can help specify for the observer the most relevant criteria for a particular program.

Of course, giving regular feedback on daily performance and conducting staff evaluations several times annually provides staff with information and techniques that prompt critical review of their own performance and the identification of training needs. However, there will be times when only the director will be able to pinpoint a specific training problem. Even so, staff should be asked for their input and be kept abreast of the training agenda. Resentment and resistance are sure byproducts of personnel who feel powerless where their own development is concerned. A training-needs form (Figure 1–3) can be useful as a secondary means of information gathering.

Once an early childhood administrator has observed and talked with all personnel, it may be apparent that a number of topics should be addressed in training sessions. If these are presented on the training-needs form and each staff member indicates a preference for the order in which these should be covered, personnel are reassured that their concerns are being considered.

It is also necessary that the program director match staff interests and needs with levels of ability, understanding, and present and future job responsibilities. Although each person should be consistently challenged by new information and ideas, the director must also be able to discern the existence of any gaps in fundamental knowledge and offer training to fill these. The administrator, coordinator, or head teacher must assume the role of resident expert in early childhood education and, as such, should be familiar with the major theories and principles of the field and the elementary, intermediate, and advanced levels of knowledge and skill appropriate for various staff positions. This leader-supervisor is responsible for matching training subjects with staff needs.

Sample topics for staff training in early childhood education follow. Each of these and many others may be dealt with at any of the aforementioned levels.

## TRAINING-NEEDS FORM
### GRANT CHILD DEVELOPMENT CENTER*

Dear Members of the Child Care Staff:

As a part of overall staff development efforts this year we will have available to us a variety of inservice and other training opportunities. Your feedback regarding training needs is essential. Please review and complete this form at your earliest convenience. I will be available to answer any questions you might have about the topics listed or procedures for filling out this survey of training needs. We will also discuss your ideas and plan a training schedule at an upcoming staff meeting.

Please return this form to my office by September 15th. Thank you for your continuing contribution to our program.

Sincerely,


Yvette Monroe
Director

*The purpose of this form is to identify specific skills, content, and methods to be developed and employed in the implementation of a training program.

FIGURE 1–3

## TRAINING-NEEDS FORM

### CHILD DEVELOPMENT CENTER

Staff Member Name: _____

Position: _____

Classroom: _____

Length of Employment at Grant Center: _____

Additional Positions Held: _____

Highest Degree Awarded: _____

Field of Study: _____

Directions: Read the list of training topics in each area. Indicate whether training in each topic would benefit staff by placing a "Y" (Yes) or "N" (No) in the first column to the left. If more than one topic is checked in each area indicate the order of importance of each topic by placing a number from one to six in the second column. A "1" indicates the most important, a "2" the second most important, etc. Then place a check in the column under "Training Activity Suggested" that best describes the form in which you think the training should be provided. For example, if you believe staff would benefit from an inservice session devoted to the topic you have selected, place a check mark under "inservice" in the column on the left-hand side of the page. Area 6 provides space for you to write in topics that you feel are missing.

| Training Topic* | Yes/No | Order of Importance | Training Activity Suggested | | | | | |
|---|---|---|---|---|---|---|---|---|
| | | | I. Inservice | II. Reading/Discussion | III. College Course | IV. Conference Attendance | V. Teacher Demonstration | VI. Staff Project |
| **Area 1: Children** | | | | | | | | |
| A. Child Development | | | | | | | | |
| B. Recognizing Abuse/ Neglect | | | | | | | | |
| C. Learning Problems | | | | | | | | |
| D. Handicapping Conditions | | | | | | | | |
| E. Gifted/Talented | | | | | | | | |
| F. Discipline/Classroom Management | | | | | | | | |

*Examples

FIGURE 1–3 cont'd.

| Training Topic* | Yes/No | Order of Importance | Training Activity Suggested | | | | | |
|---|---|---|---|---|---|---|---|---|
| | | | I. Inservice | II. Reading/Discussion | III. College Course | IV. Conference Attendance | V. Teacher Demonstration | VI. Staff Project |
| **Area 2: Families** | | | | | | | | |
| A. Parent-Child Attachment | | | | | | | | |
| B. Family Dynamics | | | | | | | | |
| C. Parent-Teacher Conferences | | | | | | | | |
| D. Parents as Volunteers | | | | | | | | |
| E. Home-School Activities | | | | | | | | |
| F. Problem Solving with Parents | | | | | | | | |
| **Area 3: Curriculum Planning** | | | | | | | | |
| A. Observation/Record Keeping | | | | | | | | |
| B. Unit Planning | | | | | | | | |
| C. Scheduling Problems | | | | | | | | |
| D. Environmental Design | | | | | | | | |
| E. Outdoor Activities | | | | | | | | |
| F. Math & Science Activities | | | | | | | | |
| **Area 4: Staff** | | | | | | | | |
| A. Managing Stress | | | | | | | | |
| B. Communication Skills | | | | | | | | |
| C. Problem Solving | | | | | | | | |
| D. Developing Partnerships | | | | | | | | |
| E. Staff Projects | | | | | | | | |
| F. Professional Growth | | | | | | | | |
| **Area 5: Community** | | | | | | | | |
| A. Identifying Resources | | | | | | | | |
| B. Field Trips | | | | | | | | |
| C. Working with Community Volunteers | | | | | | | | |
| D. Fund Raising | | | | | | | | |
| E. Editing a Newsletter | | | | | | | | |
| F. Working with Board | | | | | | | | |
| **Area 6: Write-in Section** | | | | | | | | |
| A. _____ | | | | | | | | |
| B. _____ | | | | | | | | |
| C. _____ | | | | | | | | |
| D. _____ | | | | | | | | |
| E. _____ | | | | | | | | |
| F. _____ | | | | | | | | |

*Examples

**FIGURE 1–3 cont'd.**

12

- Recognizing child abuse and neglect
- Developing classroom environments
- Programming for handicapping conditions
- Considering family issues and problems
- Planning field trips
- Developing professional partnerships
- Recognizing individual differences
- Using volunteer services
- Identifying learning problems
- Answering children's questions
- Enhancing child development
- Observing and keeping records
- Broadening language development
- Employing math/science activities
- Dealing with social-emotional problems
- Fostering home-school relations
- Planning curriculum
- Using expressive activities
- Addressing parent-child attachment
- Promoting positive behavior

## BENEFITS OF STAFF DEVELOPMENT

A comprehensive staff development component profits all of those involved in an early childhood program: administration, staff, volunteers, children, and families. Although time consuming, the exploration of staff needs and design of a plan to further professional growth are well worth any effort.

### Exchange of Information and Ideas

In order to plan and implement the staff development program, the early childhood administrator carefully scrutinizes and later keeps abreast of the talents, duties, and concerns of center personnel. Provided all are open to it, many opportunities are available for a meaningful exchange of information between staff and supervisors. Observations, staff meetings, and one-to-one conferences provide milieu in which the administrator may ascertain how staff function on a day-to-day basis, and how styles and philosophies support program goals. In addition, the director has the occasion to explore many outside staff development resources and share these with center personnel.

For the program's staff, the training component can mean the difference between job satisfaction and stress, creativity and stagnation. The support and interest shown by the director may well be the indicators to the staff that individual merit is recognized and their contributions to the center are valued. The regular exchange of ideas promotes creative thinking and activity, and even friendly competition to develop and share with the children many challenging learning situations.

## Job Satisfaction

Perhaps one of the greatest long-term benefits to staff is the sense of community and oneness of purpose that can develop over time. When everyone is involved and interested in his or her work, there is little opportunity and less inclination to gossip or dwell on personal problems. Gradually, staff become more secure about their abilities and pleased with the picture presented by the future.

## Respect for All Staff Contributions

Persons volunteering their time where staff development is a priority are viewed by paid personnel as an essential support system and a part of the team, rather than as persons who are asked to do the jobs that no one else wants. These volunteers learn along with staff because their talents and time are respected, and it is suggested that they make frequent contributions to the children's activities.

## Personal Attention to Children

The effective staff development component may ultimately be most beneficial to the children and parents that participate in the early childhood program. For the youngsters, there are opportunities for personal attention. Staff support one another, adult and child stress is avoided, and time is available for one-to-one interaction. Activities are challenging, and children are neither overtaxed nor bored. Personnel know the real meaning of "partnership," and the little ones learn about friendship, work, cooperation, and other aspects of socialization by observing their adult caregivers.

## Importance of Parents

Parents are welcome in their children's classrooms. Center personnel create many opportunities for informal exchanges about children's progress and program activities. Formal meetings are scheduled several times each school year, as staff are sensitive to the contribution that these conferences make to the programming progress. Parents are polled regarding their interests and talents, and they are encouraged to share their free time with all the children. Family members are often seen observing, participating in the children's daily routines, running errands, and planning special activities with the staff. A parents' bulletin board keeps mothers, fathers, and other visitors informed of events of interest occurring in the center and community.

## SUMMING UP

These scenarios are not too idealistic to achieve. True, much planning is needed, along with a consensus that everyone is willing to work toward staff development and other goals. This process of picturing how things might be is the first step toward creating early childhood programs that are learning centers for all.

## RECOMMENDED READING

Beegle, C. W., and R. A. Edelfelt. *Staff Development: Staff Liberation.* Alexandria, VA: Association for Supervision and Curriculum Development, 1977.

Dillon-Petterson, B. (ed.) *Staff Development/Organizational Development,* 1981 Yearbook. Alexandria, VA: Association for Supervision and Curriculum Development, 1981.

Galloway, C. M. (ed.), "Teacher Development: Personal and Professional Growth," *Theory into Practice,* Vol. XIX, No. 4, Autumn 1980.

Gordon, T. *Leader Effectiveness Training: L.E.T.* New York: Bantam Books, 1978.

Joyce, B. R., and B. Showers. *Power in Staff Development Through Research on Training.* Alexandria, VA: Association for Supervision and Curriculum Development, 1983.

Watkins, L. G. "I have an idea! Let's have a suggestion box!," *Educational Leadership,* Vol. 42, No. 4, December 1984/January 1985, pp. 36–37.

## CHAPTER 1 NOTES

1. J. Goodlad, "The Resistance of Schools to Change" (Audiotape), Educational Resources Associations, 1972.

2. B. A. Farber and J. Miller, "Teacher Burnout: A Psychoeducational Perspective," *Teachers College Record*, Vol. 83, No. 2, Winter 1981.

3. Bank Street College of Education oversees the Child Development Associate Credential Award System. This system for child-care worker assessment includes thirteen different criteria areas describing caregiver skills.

# CHAPTER 2

# Styles for Staff Development Leadership

*"Leadership is many things...It is patient...It's building a loyal team...that speaks more or less with one voice. It's listening carefully much of the time, frequently speaking with encouragement, and reinforcing words with believable action."*[1]

FOR A RARE group of individuals, leadership appears to be an innate ability, manifesting itself in the games of early childhood. For the majority, however, there is a slow realization of the ability to motivate, plan, and direct individuals and situations. Rarely are we taught the skills that make effective leadership a reality; rather the learning occurs by trial and error, or sometimes by observing th right mentor. Unfortunately, once appointed the director of an early childhood center, you work with the staff and make decisions with little time for trial-and-error learning. Serious mistakes in judgment can extract a heavy price from the program, children, and personnel. For this reason, this chapter is about leadership and about the styles and techniques most conducive to staff development. If early childhood directors can look clearly at themselves, determine the skills they have as well as those they would like to develop, then many kinds of changes—and higher-quality programs—become possible.

## EVOLUTION OF LEADERSHIP STYLES

Leadership characteristics are somewhat elusive. We sometimes say that leaders are "charismatic," because we have difficulty identifying exactly what it is about some individuals that causes us to follow, imitate, and defer to them. We also have learned from history that leadership does not necessarily mean that a person is virtuous or moral. Leaders do, however, tend to be powerful persons who have authority to make rules that others are expected to follow. Leaders can be creators or destroyers, depending upon their style and goals, on whether they nurture or stifle those who follow them.

How does a style of leadership evolve? Early influences probably occur in childhood when authority figures appear in the form of parents and teachers. As observers of young children, we often see youngsters mimicking parental behavior and play-acting various discipline measures during dramatic play. In middle childhood our teachers are influential. In adolescence, we take note of movie and television heroes, literary characters, and peers. We begin to formulate ideas about what one has to do to win, to achieve goals. If we are to be leaders we learn to utilize those behaviors and gradually develop winning techniques of our own. If we succeed as a trendsetter, in style of dress, the way we wear our hair, or the number of sports points won, this adds to our notion of leadership. People watch us with admiration and sometimes imitate us. We have begun to have an idea of what constitutes a leader. Of course, education, experience, and the maturity of adulthood refine and mold early ideas.

By the time they assume an administrative position in early childhood education, many directors already have a sense of the kind of leader they want to be. They may even have exercised some leadership skills as a teacher in an early childhood classroom. All of this is to say that we begin developing and practicing our leadership potential long before we sit behind the director's desk.

## LEADERSHIP STYLES FOR DIRECTORS

Although no individual exactly fits any behavioral mold, leadership styles have been studied and grouped into three general types: the autocratic, democratic, and the laissez-faire.[2]

### The Autocratic Leader

Autocratic leadership is a control-oriented style of management. The autocratic director is the creator and interpreter of all guidelines followed by the staff. This individual closely monitors all of the activities of the program and provides subjective feedback as needed. The autocratic leader interprets job descriptions strictly and expects personnel to understand and follow these closely. When problems arise, the autocratic leader has identified specific procedures to be followed and accepts ultimate responsibility for any decisions that result. Appropriate behavior and activity are rewarded by this director, and all personnel are aware when displeasure has been incurred. Autocratic leaders are goal-oriented, and the efforts of administrators, staff, and involved parents are all focused on clearly stated aims.

### The Democratic Leader

The second of common styles of leadership is called democratic. Its focus, invariably, is on participation in decision making and sharing of overall responsibility by the staff. The democratic director demonstrates flexibility with regard to staff roles, often working together or exchanging duties with other personnel. This administrator seeks input and utilizes staff expertise wherever it exists. While conducting regular evaluations of personnel, a democratic leader also requests feedback from staff regarding the effectiveness of administration. Although this leader provides guidelines for personnel, rules are more flexibly enforced. This is a process-oriented style of management, tuned in to those people who make the process work.

## The Laissez-Faire Leader

Third of the management styles is called the laissez-faire approach. It is a more relaxed style often without obvious goals. Laissez-faire directors do not demonstrate consistency with regard to their own or the responsibilities of other staff and may even avoid involvement in administrative functions. Policies and procedures may be somewhat unclear to program participants. There may be few or irregular evaluations of staff and program, and suggestions for improvement are probably infrequent. Significant contributions and inappropriate activities may be equally ignored, for neither praise nor punishment are common occurrences. This leadership style works only when staff are self-motivated and very independent.

## A Combination of All Three Styles

As previously stated, few directors fit precisely into one of the three categories. In reality, most directors, depending on the situation and a variety of factors, may exhibit the characteristics of any one of these three styles. For this reason, it is important to recognize the type of behavior associated with each leadership style and to be conscious of its effects on staff and children. An early childhood director must evaluate every problem as extensively as time permits in order to choose a response style of management appropriate to the problem. The following suggestions are offered for choosing the leadership style that suits the situation:

- Avoid speaking hastily. Think carefully and speak slowly when responding to questions or situations for which there is no established policy.

- Keep strong emotions in check. Loss of emotional control usually means a corresponding loss of objectivity.

- Maintain familiarity with the philosophy and aims of the program. Utilize these as criteria in decision-making situations. Evaluate situations in light of their impact on program goals.

- When personnel problems arise, avoid focusing on personalities involved. Deal with the issues and evolve solutions that create the least amount of conflict between individuals.

- Seek input, whenever possible, from individuals who are involved or will be affected by decisions made (children, parents, staff, board, community).

- When lacking expertise to make an informed decision, seek outside assistance. It is better to delay an important decision temporarily than to make one without considering all factors and people involved.

- Plan carefully for all program activities, then consider possible alternatives. The more contingency plans that are available, the more likely operations will run smoothly, and abrupt, inappropriate decisions will be avoided.

- Do not hesitate to use authority when it seems the appropriate thing to do. Ultimately, responsibility for the program rests with the director, and even when other input is sought the program's administrator must have the final word.

## LEADERSHIP FOR STAFF GROWTH

What are the management factors that motivate staff development? They may be divided into two categories: direct and indirect. By this is meant that some staff growth occurs as a result of purposive efforts and plans to facilitate personnel development, such as personnel evaluations and inservice training.

Unfortunately, many directors are unaware of the "indirect" factors that impact on staff. That is, many managerial techniques give strong messages that either promote or restrict personal and professional growth of staff. Examples of indirect factors include the director's day-to-day behaviors, activities, language, and responses to daily events. These messages are often the most powerful, though indirect, indicators that developing as a person and as a caregiver is an appropriate or inappropriate activity.

The following situations illustrate the direct and indirect influences that may be exerted upon your staff's professional growth.

> When Marian L. became the director of a child development center, she was determined to encourage staff development. Having been a classroom teacher for many years, Marian had worked under several program managers who appeared unconcerned with professional growth of staff. There had been little inservice training, no solicitation of staff feedback or suggestions, no opportunities for attendance at conferences or outside workshops. Marian has a keen understanding of the sense of frustration caregivers experience when there is little chance for advancement. She almost left the early childhood profession while a teacher when her enthusiasm dwindled and her stress level increased. Marian was committed to a different type of leadership for her own staff. After discussions with all personnel about their needs, and following a series of classroom observations, Marian designed staff development goals for the program plan. In addition, she sought input from several of her former college professors regarding ways to stimulate staff interest in the program. She sought and received funds to enable staff to enroll in college courses and scheduled a series of inservice training sessions.

Marian's approach is a direct one. She has identified for the staff a set of goals aimed at motivating overall personnel growth and has designed a series of activities to achieve staff development aims.

There is a second approach that directors may choose. It is the one referred to as "indirect," and is described in the following scenario:

> Richard W. is a primary-school principal. Like Marian, Richard is convinced that staff development is an important aspect of high-quality early childhood programming. He provides substitute coverage so that classroom teachers may attend many types of professional activities. Richard maintains both an open-door policy and a staff suggestion box. Teachers' ideas are shared at each staff meeting and, suggestions are often adopted. Richard is, himself, a student in a graduate program. He regularly shares information learned at the university with his staff. When working in his office at school, Richard wears business clothing. Without talking down to staff or parents, he uses appropriate language, being careful to avoid academic jargon. Richard is aware of the boundaries of professional ethics and observes them at all times.

Richard utilizes both direct and indirect methods to stimulate professional development. On one hand, he is aware of the need for goals and direction, the sort of guidelines that enable effective operation of program components. Richard is also successfully using indirect tools to achieve the same ends. His techniques include role modeling for his staff, who see Richard involved in the same activities in which he urges them to participate. He demonstrates the qualities and competencies that the staff are encouraged to develop. Because Richard is both liked and respected, his example has an enormous impact on the personnel in his school.

Both of these approaches are appropriate. Problems arise, however, when despite the creation and implementation of appropriate plans, directors fail to realize that staff are observing to see if management practices what it preaches.

When observing in day-care centers, we often see posted rules for children stating "Do not sit on the table" or "Keep indoor voices low." Although teachers are frequently reminding children to follow these guidelines, the teachers themselves sit on the tables and talk in loud voices. Those same teachers wonder why they have classroom management problems. So it is for managers. The staff takes the cues for appropriate behavior from their director. In short, it is much easier to maintain a developmental environment and involve staff in growth-related activities if the director is growing and learning.

In the next section of this chapter we will explore two different roles that the director can play in relation to growth-seeking caregivers.

## DIRECTORS AS MENTORS

College courses in administration have not been developed that teach the skills learned from practical experience. An additional difficulty is that early childhood leaders seldom have the means to look in a truly objective fashion at what they do during the inservice learning period. The consequences are that learning sometimes results from a series of errors that can cause many hours of self-recrimination.

The early childhood director has the opportunity to offer an aspiring leader direction, support, and feedback. In an apprenticeship-type arrangement, a director can be available to provide the experiences and behavior modeling that enable the developing professional to benefit from the knowledge and skills of another. We refer to this special relationship as a mentorship.

Becoming a mentor to a member of the early childhood staff is not unlike becoming a tutor. It is a one-to-one staff development program with unique aims. Although early childhood administrators often influence staff in informal ways, using techniques that personnel are not always aware of, the assumption of the mentorship role is deliberate activities on the part of both "teacher" and "learner." Both parties are conscious of their roles and agree to them.

Mentorship is generally undertaken in one of two ways. An aspiring leader must identify with the program director in some fashion. That identification sometimes comes from similarity in backgrounds, or from the admiration of the apprentice for the abilities of the administrator. There is often the strong desire to follow in the footsteps of the mentor.

This relationship can also be generated by a leader's recognition of hidden talents and pursuit of a professionally undernourished member of the staff. Regardless of the manner in which a mentorship originates, the key to its success is that the individuals involved have an acknowledged professional need for one another. Many directors achieve a great sense of satisfaction from the knowledge that they have nurtured the development of a talented co-worker. The apprentice has the chance to go beyond theories and discussion to observation and practice alongside a successful early childhood administrator.

## The Roles and Tasks of Successful Mentorship

Effective mentorship requires that a leader play a variety of roles in relationship to an apprentice. These roles enable the learner to observe, practice, make mistakes, and eventually master important skills. Examples include:

| | |
|---|---|
| *Role model* | The mentor demonstrates for the apprentice appropriate leadership styles and behaviors in response to everyday situations and unique management situations |
| *Teacher* | The mentor introduces, discusses, and illustrates theories, concepts, and skills, heretofore unfamiliar to the apprentice |
| *Critic* | The mentor provides appropriate feedback relative to the practice of teaching/caregiving competencies and leadership skills |

| | |
|---|---|
| *Collaborator* | The mentor and apprentice work together to develop, implement, and evaluate ideas, programs, and projects |
| *Confessor* | The mentor is available to listen to and provide feedback regarding the concerns, problems, and needs of the apprentice, as these are relative to the goals of mentorship |
| *Supporter* | The mentor provides unqualified encouragement for the appropriate efforts of the apprentice to develop leadership skills and achieve predetermined goals |

## Mentorship Concerns

The mentor's role must be consistently assessed to determine its impact and direction. Like any well-intentioned staff development effort, mentorship can go awry and even become a program-damaging element. A director-mentor must determine the impact of the mentorship relationship on the rest of the staff. Often mentor and apprentice develop a close, personal friendship, which may be incorrectly interpreted by other personnel. This misunderstanding can be further complicated if racial or sexual (male/female) differences exist between mentor and apprentice. Furthermore, staff may feel that the mentorship deprives them of opportunities for growth. Therefore, it is essential for a mentoring director to give all personnel clear options for professional development.

Yet another complication of the mentorship relationship deals with the apprentice's failure to develop independence and self-motivated direction. Although friendships that originate as mentorship-apprentice ties often last for many years beyond the needs for teaching, there should be an early emergence of a pattern of independent learning on the part of the leader-in-training. No mentor should feel indefinitely, uncomfortably tied to an apprentice.

Lastly, the director should have a clear sense of the value of the role and its return for him or her. Leadership makes enormous demands of time and energy on an individual. Assuming a mentorship is another responsibility, one that can be tremendously taxing or extremely rewarding. An apprentice can also be a supporter, collaborator, and colleague, giving as well as taking through the teaching process. A director must establish the parameters and goals of mentorship before making an investment and must have an understanding of personal and professional needs to be addressed via mentoring.

## THE PARTNERSHIP MODEL

While many directors prefer a teacher-learner style of implementing staff development activities, there is another approach to be considered. Many democratic-style leaders experience discomfort when considering taking the route where they must assume control of and responsibility for the professional growth of staff. They prefer to assume a role more equal or parallel to that of those they manage, a partnership approach. This is not difficult to understand. In many early childhood programs, especially those that are privately run or community funded, directors are not significantly better educated nor more experienced than their staff. It is also common for directors to rise from the staff ranks to assume their leadership positions. A sudden change in role, demeanor, and relationship may be unfamiliar and uncomfortable for all parties.

A partnership[3] style of staff development may also be favored by an experienced director-staff developer. We have observed that while teacher-training institutions devote significant time to preparing individuals to work with children, little effort goes into facilitating skills that enable adults to work, cooperate, and learn together—a significant factor in the success of early childhood programs. Trained teachers leave college classrooms filled with ideas for lessons and activities, materials and equipment, and environmental design. They soon discover, however, that many of the problems and pitfalls lie at the root of the staff interactions and individual needs for "belongingness, esteem, and self-actualization."[4] The partnership model for early childhood staff development can provide an alternative approach for leaders who have raised these issues and expressed such concerns.

## The Partnership Concept

What is the partnership model, and how does it operate? Partnership is first and foremost based upon equality. For many years, due primarily to male-dominance within the business community, cooperative personnel efforts have been spoken of as "teamwork." Teamwork implies interdependence, loyalty, and common aims. But in reality, players on the corporate team often function in different ways and reap very different outcomes for their efforts. Some team players may not have a chance to play at all. They may be forced to be benchwarmers because those with specific expertise are busy demonstrating their skills and developing positions of power. It is the very nature of team activity that persons are expected to spend time developing and promoting their individual abilities. This is a sensible approach on the playing field, perhaps even in the boardroom, where strong competition among team players is an accepted and appropriate measure of ambition.

However, the early childhood classroom is a very inappropriate setting for such competition. Some competition is a necessary and even healthy motivator of human drive and energies, but competition out of control is a dangerous and destructive force. The partnership model minimizes competitive forces and focuses group and individual efforts on common goals, interests, and experiences. While there is room for leadership within a partnership, it is essential that such direction be democratic in nature. In this fashion, the interests and needs of the group as well as individuals remain at the forefront.

## Partnership and Power

Many human service workers experience job burnout. Barry Farber of Columbia University has attributed the high rate of burnout among teachers to those unstudied factors that "…lead to a lack of psychological sense of community—a lack that produces feelings on the part of teachers of both isolation and inconsequentiality."[5] One might say that in some respects burnout is related to the sense of loss of power. In many early childhood settings, especially in day-care centers, power becomes a powerful asset. Caregivers achieve status who have good classroom management skills, can influence parents, give accepted input to directors, and are attending degree programs— all indicators of power in the day-care milieu. A sense of inequality frustrates and isolates the "powerless" and may contribute to many kinds of personnel problems.

Partnership focuses on elevating all staff members to similar positions of esteem within the group. The development needs of all members can, therefore, be recognized and responded to. No one is left powerless.

## Forming an Early Childhood Partnership

It is important to note that partnerships do not materialize in some accidental fashion. Their formation is always deliberate, carefully considered, and has willing participants. No one is ever coerced into partnership association.

If a director wishes to introduce the possibility of a staff partnership, several prerequisites need to be in place. First, there would be a consensus that change was needed in the staff development component. Second, staff would be ready to make a commitment to some avenue for overall program development. Third, the director would have some idea what the staff training and development needs are and would have created a plan for implementation. At that point, personnel could sit down together to formulate the parameters, components, and timetable for their partnership.

## Components of Partnership

Although each partnership is unique in accordance with its membership, goals, interests, and expertise, there are certain basic elements of agreement essential for partnership success.[6]

- *Common Goals*—partners must agree upon the common purposes of their association, as well as the staff development outcomes it is hoped that partnership will produce.

- *Common Language*—partners agree to avoid use of the cultural or academic jargon that can separate associates. Key language used by partners must be examined and meanings agreed upon.

- *Shared Experience*—involves agreement by partners to share their individual, professionally enriching experiences, as well as to create opportunities for the partners to be involved together in staff development activities, such as group conference attendance.

- *Established Systems of Communication*—since communications failures are at the heart of many personnel problems, it is essential for partners to identify their communications needs and the techniques and occasions for conveying information to one another.

- *Respect for Individual Strengths/Acceptance of Weaknesses*—acknowledgment of each partner's uniqueness and willingness to defer to the expertise of others is an essential partnership component.

- *Shared Responsibility for Successes and Failures*—partners must acknowledge that not all plans and programs are successful. A critical ingredient of successful partnership is sharing the credit for success and avoiding blame placing.

- *Loyalty to the Partnership*—this may well be the key component for a winning partnership. It involves commitment to the group's goals and the idea of placing the good of the partnership before individual concerns, in most circumstances.

- *Agreement to Disagree/Compromise*—partners must be willing to disagree without sacrificing the group and to compromise when there is no winning point. It is a significant step in professional development to recognize that growth can emerge from compromise.

- *Equal Contributions over Time*—each partner must have opportunity to make contributions he or she is comfortable with. No one partner should feel that he or she contributes significantly more than the others.

- *Agreement on the Type and Frequency of Partnership Evaluations*—all partnerships require regular assessment to determine whether group goals and individual satisfaction are being achieved. Goals also need regular updating. New partners will periodically be admitted to the association, causing changes in the way partners interact and introducing new conditions and situations requiring evaluation into the relationship.

## SUMMING UP

Leadership styles are as unique as the persons who hold leadership positions. There is room for every director, principal, and program coordinator to establish his or her own effective means to guide staff development through one or a combination of several effective approaches. Leaders must, however, stay attuned to individual group staff functioning. The staying-in-touch process is essential in order for directors to gauge the effectiveness and direction of their leadership styles.

## RECOMMENDED READING

Cozier, E., et al., "Master of All Trades: The Skills of Facilitators," *Training News*, April 1984, pp. 12–13.

Deal, T., and A. A. Kennedy. *Corporate Cultures: The Rites and Rituals of Corporate Life.* (Reading, MA: Addison-Wesley Publishing Company, 1982).

Gordon, T. *Leadership Effectiveness Training: L.E.T.* (New York: Bantam Books, 1978).

Katz, L. G., and E. H. Ward. *Ethical Behavior in Early Childhood Education.* Washington, DC.: National Association for the Education of Young Children, 1978).

Streets, D. F. *Administering Day Care And Preschool Programs.* (Boston: Allyn and Bacon, Inc., 1982).

Travis, W., and J. Perreault. *Day Care Personnel Management.* (Atlanta, GA: Southern Regional Education Board, 1979).

White, R., and R. Lippitt, "Leadership Behavior and Member Reaction in Three Social Climates," in eds. C. Cartwright and and A. Zander. *Group Dynamics.* (New York: Row, Peterson Publishers, 1953), pp. 585–611.

## CHAPTER 2 NOTES

1. T. J. Peters and R. H. Waterman, Jr. *In Search of Excellence: Lessons from America's Best Run Companies.* New York: Harper and Row, Publishers, Inc., 1982.

2. R. White and R. Lippitt, "Leadership Behavior and Member Reaction in Three 'Social Climates,'" in *Group Dynamics*, eds. R. White and R. Lippitt. New York: Row, Peterson, 1953.

3. L. Durant and K. Watkins, "Developing Professional Partnerships in Early Childhood Settings," in *Target I*, Vol. 2, Part II, ed. Marian Taylor Giles. Amarillo, TX: Teaching Pathways, Inc., 1983, pp. 221–230.

4. A. H. Maslow, *Motivation and Personality.* New York: Harper and Row, 1954.

5. B. A. Farber and J. Miller, "Teacher Burnout: A Psychoeducational Perspective," in *Teachers College Record*, Vol. 83, No. 2, Winter 1981, p. 238.

6. L. Durant and K. Watkins, ibid.

# CHAPTER 3

## Staff Development As a Tool to Motivate Change

WHEREVER HUMAN service is the focus of activity, change is not only possible, but is likely to be frequent. The essence of change is movement, movement that is "planned, controlled, and purposive."[1] When the need for change is indicated or when change occurs abruptly there is always an uncertain degree of impact, as some effects are obvious while others are far less apparent. To suggest that change affects only programs is incorrect, for change primarily concerns the people who create it and foster its completion. In this chapter, the change process will be examined in the light of its influences on early childhood staff and their needs for inservice education and other forms of staff development activity.

What factors motivate change in early childhood centers? Close examination of programs suggests that change usually originates with one or several of the groups involved in providing or receiving services (the administrators, staff, volunteers, children, parents, and the community-at-large). The need for change may be noticed only gradually, or it may be immediately apparent due to some sudden and unforeseen circumstances.

The following are some examples of situations, occurring in relation to various early childhood personnel and program clients, that can be the forerunners of change:

## Administration

- A day-care center administrator receives a directive from the program's advisory board to upgrade the curriculum offered to the children.
- A new director is hired who has plans to revamp the program of the child development center.
- The school principal attends a conference on Montessori education and decides that Montessori materials and activities should be adapted for use in the school's kindergarten classrooms.
- A mandate is issued that directs federally funded early childhood programs to accept 15 percent handicapped children into their classrooms.
- The board of education requires early childhood centers to begin using computers for all record-keeping procedures.

## Staff

- One of the preschool classroom teachers receives a master's degree in early childhood education.
- A teacher's aide enrolls in child development classes at a local community college.
- A new head teacher is hired who will oversee all curriculum development for the day-care center.
- By mutual agreement, the morning and afternoon kindergarten teachers will exchange classroom aides.
- The cook/nutritionist for the day-care center has asked to be more involved in the children's activities.

## Volunteers

- The preschool director has developed linkages with a local senior center, and several older adults will be assigned to participate in the children's program.
- The school principal is contacted by the chairperson of a local college's early childhood department, who wishes to place students in first- and second-grade classrooms for practicum experience.
- A neighborhood child development center has been relocated to a nearby high school, and junior and senior students will begin working with the younger children as a laboratory experience requirement for a child-psychology class.
- The day-care center director wishes to develop a volunteer orientation program.
- An established preschool program changes its policy to permit parents to work cooperatively with classroom teachers in lieu of paying higher fees for services.

## Children

- Several children in a first-grade classroom are diagnosed as learning disabled, a problem with which their teachers have had no previous experience.
- Several newly immigrated Vietnamese families enroll their children in the local day-care center. There are no Vietnamese staff at the center.
- The school nurse discovers that a kindergarten child has been sexually abused by her uncle.

- A preschool child returns to school after a long absence due to serious illness.
- A child development center plans to expand to include a kindergarten program along with regular preschool services.

## Parents

- It is noted by staff that a high percentage of youngsters in their child development center come from families where parents are divorced or separated.
- Although attendance at home-school meetings has been low, many parents have suggested to staff that they would like to be more involved in their children's child-care program.
- Parents attending a home-school meeting ask many questions and request a number of changes in the school curriculum.
- A new policy instituted by the day-care-center advisory board allows parents to observe in classrooms merely by signing in at the center office.
- Several parents have voiced concern regarding the nursery school teachers' handling of children's behavior problems and have met with the school's director asking for a resolution of the problem.

### IMPLICATIONS OF THE NEED FOR CHANGE

The aforementioned situations are the sort that occur every day in early childhood centers across the country. Furthermore, these indicators of approaching change carry with them a number of implications.

## Implication #1

All of these situations will *require an alteration of at least one component of the existing program.* The director who is told by the day-care-center advisory board to modify the curriculum will be facing changes in the children's program, staff development, and parent-education areas.

## Implication #2

All of these situations *require the involvement of several different groups of individuals participating in the program.* The cook/nutritionist who wants to be more active in the children's program will need the support of other staff members, children, parents, and administration in order to accomplish this goal.

## Implication #3

Each of the sample situations *requires some degree of decision making.* While vital determinations are generally made at administrative levels, there are others whose input is equally important to the success of the intended change.

If some center children are identified as learning disabled the school will be required by law (Public Law 94–142) to provide an individualized educational program (IEP) designed specifically for each youngster. To achieve this end, parents, teachers, psychologists, health-care personnel, bus drivers, and others must be consulted. Whenever possible, the children themselves should participate as the learning objectives are developed to meet their needs.

## Implication #4

Every situation *means some sort of adjustment, at times physical, emotional or social,* that persons involved in the program must make.

When center policies are redesigned to permit parents free access to their youngsters' classrooms for purposes of observation, all must become accustomed to the changes that accompany new levels of parent involvement. Parents will only gradually become familiar with the daily schedule and elements of the curriculum appropriate for their children. At first, parents' ideas of what their youngsters should be learning may be radically different from what they observe. Teachers and other staff will need time to become comfortable with parental presence in the classroom and the many types of feedback that can result from this new activity.

For the children, adjustment may be the most difficult and problematic. Even the child who greatly enjoys school may experience a resurgence of old insecurities when a parent is present. The youngster's discomfort may be increased if parents are invited to be involved in activities, and the child sees his or her parent interacting with other boys and girls. As most early childhood professionals are aware, children may also have home and school behaviors that vary greatly. For some children, seeing teachers, parents, and school friends together in the same setting may at first be confusing.

## Implication #5

Yet another of the implications of those situations that promote change is that the vast majority will *need to be addressed through staff training.* That is, all personnel will need to come together to receive information and discuss the questions, issues, and modifications to come. Even the roles of various staff may require redefinition or broadening.

One thing is certain: unless these issues are presented, opportunities for discussion are provided, and resolutions are found, change cannot be successful. In these cases, children are usually the ones most negatively affected.

## THE ROLE OF STAFF DEVELOPMENT IN THE CHANGE PROCESS

When change is in the offing, many early childhood staff justly feel that they are the last to be informed. Events about to take place will affect the staff's job responsibilities, sense of security, and satisfaction with work performed. Yet decisions that will affect those who work with the children are often made by persons who are not directly involved in the classroom. It is little wonder that these determinations sometimes invite the resentment and uncooperativeness of the center's personnel.

However, staff unwillingness to accept new things is not a necessary condition of change. Change can be made palatable, even welcome, through careful preparation and appropriate use of inservice training and other staff development resources. Such activities become the vehicles through which modification of programs can be effectively and successfully accomplished, but only if administrators are willing to accept staff as partners in the change process.

At this point, some comparison of the early childhood center and other types of businesses is appropriate. If one partner in a business fails to inform the other of critical financial, personnel, or product-production matters, the entire operation can fall to ruin. Therefore, partners must talk regularly with one another, consult before making strategic moves, and plan for these changes carefully.

In the early childhood program, the inservice meeting or training session becomes the forum for many similar interactions. Viewed in light of its potential as a change agent, staff development activities of many kinds become an essential tool of the early childhood administrator.

In order to examine the interrelationship and dependency of aspects of staff development and the process of change, it may be helpful to follow step by step as several of the previously described situations reach appropriate conclusions and affect intended changes. It is important to remember that those presented are not the only possible solutions, but are ones likely to help all involved make a more comfortable adjustment to new ideas and experiences.

### Situation A

The school principal attends a conference on Montessori education and decides that Montessori materials and activities should be adapted for use in the school's kindergarten classroom.

*Step 1*    Assuming that the principal was not previously familiar with Montessori philosophy and techniques, the administrator should undertake additional research into this approach prior to presenting the idea to the staff. Professional reading and observations in other schools that use the Montessori approach would be an effective way to begin.

*Step 2*     Satisfied that such a change is both feasible and appropriate, the principal might check personnel files for indications that staff have had Montessori training or classroom experiences.

*Step 3*     Choosing the occasion carefully, the principal would introduce to the kindergarten teachers and their aides the concept of adding a Montessori component to the curriculum, asking for their feedback and suggestions for possible implementation.

*Step 4*     The principal would discuss the plan for the new curriculum at a meeting with the entire teaching staff. Questions would be welcomed, and the kindergarten staff would help to answer these. Prior to the meeting, the principal and kindergarten teachers would have brainstormed possible staff concerns.

*Step 5*     Teachers in the kindergarten classrooms would receive release time to observe in Montessori schools. Montessori trained teachers would be invited to visit the school and meet with the kindergarten staff.

*Step 6*     Workshops on Montessori philosophy, lessons, and materials would be planned for kindergarten teachers and aides. The principal would attend these sessions, and the inservice sessions would likewise be open to other staff.

*Step 7*     Kindergarten teachers would be asked to help select the Montessori materials that may be purchased on a predetermined budget. Working together with their aides, the teachers create and display large floor plans showing the environmental effects of the intended change.

*Step 8*     The impending change (to be implemented during the summer months) is revealed to parents in a home-school meeting. Parents' questions are answered and options discussed for families who feel that they may not want their youngsters to participate in the new curriculum.

In Situation A, several types of staff development activities would be instrumental in stimulating, examining, and affecting the change to a Montessori influenced curriculum. The administrator of the school attended a professional conference, read related materials, and observed in model school settings. Staff participated in the change process by meeting in both small and large groups to discuss the issues, by conducting outside observations, by completing small projects, and through investment in inservice education programs.

How does this approach to change affect its success? First, none of the involved parties would be excluded from this program development activity. Although the principal determines that change is in order, the school staff receive many indications of both the need for and value of their input. The change is introduced in the manner of a suggestion, rather than as a nondebatable directive. Personnel have opportunities to explore the nature and impact of the new curriculum and raise legitimate concerns before the change plan goes into operation. Unit partners are encouraged to organize and consider how they might implement the change, and these same staff are invited to present the new idea to other school personnel and eventually to the parents. Although steps like these cannot guarantee the acceptance of change, they have been known to make the transition more pleasant for everyone.

## Situation B

The preschool center director has contact with the local senior citizens' center, and several older adults will be assigned to participate in the children's program.

*Step 1*     After introducing the idea of volunteer grandparent workers to the staff, a representative from the senior center is invited to talk with personnel and answer their questions.

*Step 2*     Several members of the staff are asked to visit another local preschool program that utilizes senior volunteers and to report their findings at the next staff meeting. Other staff are provided with articles on successful senior volunteer projects in other parts of the country. They will report to the rest of the staff on current research findings. Some teaching personnel will be working with the director to develop a volunteer orientation program.

*Step 3*     All of the volunteers from the senior center participate in three days of orientation prior to beginning work at the preschool center. Staff rotate work shifts so that all can be present for some of these sessions. Each staff member acts as a trainer for some aspect of the orientation program, thereby helping to familiarize volunteers with staff names and roles.

The knowledgeable director in Situation B helped to assure the success of this change in several ways. First, by acknowledging that staff would have many questions and sending people out to find their own answers, this issue was effectively and quickly dealt with. Second, although this director made all final decisions, the school's personnel were involved in many others. Staff helped to prepare for the senior volunteers in many ways, including determining the kinds of information that the older adults would need. The research papers some staff read also served to acquaint them with the many benefits of adding the "grandparent component" to the program.

The next scenario looks at still another type of change and the positive effects of staff development activity.

## Situation C

Several parents have voiced concern regarding the nursery school teachers' handling of children's behavior problems and have discussed these concerns with the school's director asking for a resolution of the problem.

This situation is rather different from the others previously discussed. At first glance, it may appear that there is a challenge as to the competence of the school's personnel. Some staff may respond defensively, feeling that parents do not respect their training and skills. In fact, a challenge is presented, but not that one of questioning staff credentials. This challenge involves a test of the staff's ability to be good listeners—to hear both the voiced parental concerns and those feelings that go unmentioned. Staff will have to listen as objectively as possible, with recognition and acceptance of the fact that the existence of parents' questions indicates that some sort of change is in order. Finally, the director and teachers will have to determine which of the parental concerns are justified, the areas in which change is needed, and the techniques for bringing change about. Some possible responses to this situation follow:

*Step 1*     During a meeting in the school office, the director listens carefully to parents' concerns about staff handling of their children's behavior problems. Although sympathetic, the director resists any inclination to be defensive or critical of staff methods. The director assures parents that the situation will be looked into and promises to meet with them again in one week's time.

*Step 2*     The director calls a meeting of all teaching/caregiving personnel. The parents' concerns are presented as a problem that all staff will have to work on together. No one is faulted for mishandling children's discipline. Teachers are asked to write short observation-based reports on the children in question and the staff's ordinary manner of responding to them. The director arranges to observe in these classrooms. All brainstorm regarding ways to improve home-school communications, especially with regard to clarifying program policies on discipline.

*Step 3*     The director arranges for a staff inservice on behavior management techniques in order to provide new ideas for handling discipline problems.

*Step 4*     The director and parents meet a second time, and parents are again reassured of the staff's desire to work closely with them.

Existing policies for behavior management are reviewed. Several of the steps taken by the director in responding to their concerns are discussed, including the staff meeting, observations, and inservice. Steps for improving parent-teacher communications are outlined, and parents are urged to make appointments to meet privately with their children's teachers. The director asks to meet again with parents in one month's time.

Home-school communication problems are not "solved" when steps like these are followed. Rather, these represent only the beginning of change that will occur over some period of time. Parents' complaints were a signal that something in the school's system of communications was malfunctioning. When first concerned about their children, parents should have felt comfortable to talk with their youngsters' teachers. Instead they chose to talk among themselves, as was signified by the fact that several parents came to the director together. The teachers were totally bypassed. In order to respond to this and less apparent problems, time and patience are needed.

Part of the staff development process involves helping individuals to develop introspective capabilities. Situation C presents an opportunity for such activity as it should occur in the earliest stages of professional growth. That is, it is often easier for staff to look at their shortcomings as a group, than it is for individuals to self-evaluate. In resolving this situation, the director presented and modeled techniques, and it is to be hoped that staff members will utilize them at a later point, for analyzing personal strengths and weaknesses.

An aspect of staff development rarely discussed is one related to the role of loyalty to others on the early childhood team. The director in this situation also provided an example of *esprit de corps* by finding an approach to address parental concerns without the need for a staff scapegoat.

Had the director failed to see this situation as an opportunity for change, the end result might have been quite different. Staff might have felt betrayed by their supervisor and singled out to bear responsibility for the problem. Furthermore, parents would be justified in removing their youngsters from a center where they felt that interest in their own and their children's needs was absent. An administrator's first response to potential problems will often make the difference between long-term difficulty and a change that benefits everyone.

## GUIDELINES FOR ACHIEVING CHANGE

Guidelines that may enable the early childhood administrator to use a staff development approach to achieve change include:

- Make the procedures for airing and resolving problems clear to everyone (staff and families) involved in the program.

- Observe and listen to identify staff needs. Remember that not everyone can express feelings openly. Some will need assistance and opportunity to make their needs known.

- Use discretion when handling staff and parents' problems. All should be able to rely on the director to be loyal and treat personal conversations with discretion.

- Remain open to suggestions. A director is a leader and facilitator, but should not be a dictator. Many ideas that can improve program quality often come from staff, parents, and children.

- Encourage staff involvement in activities outside the center. If welcomed, each developmental step made by school personnel represents potential growth for all in the program.

- Create frequent learning opportunities on-site through inservice, special programs, and staff projects.

- Whenever possible, utilize staff members to assist in carrying out various administrative duties. At the same time, make regular working appearances in the classroom. Provide each person with responsibilities and feedback that let all know that they are needed and appreciated.

- Avoid any tendency to view persons or situations as being completely negative. Investigate possibilities for improving staff competence and program quality through whatever situations arise.

- Keep abreast of new methods, approaches, and current research in the early childhood field. Share this information with staff, and in consultation with them seek ways to apply it to program components.

- Remember that an administrator is constantly looked to as a model for staff and parents and that he or she is expected to set the tone for the manner in which adults and children interact together.

## SUMMING UP

When programs reach a certain point in development and remain there, they become stagnant. People, their lifestyles, needs, and the community they live in are constantly changing. The early childhood center must have a staff that is aware of and reflects those differences. No program meets all needs or represents the perfect approach to programming for young children. If, however, staff are encouraged toward professional development, and if they are treated as partners in the teaching-learning process, then change and growth are infinitely possible.

## RECOMMENDED READING

Baldridge, J. V., and T. Deal. *Managing Change in Educational Organizations.* Berkeley, CA: McCutchan Publishers, 1975.

Culver, C., and G. Hoban. *The Power to Change: Issues for the Innovative Educator.* New York: McGraw-Hill Co., 1973.

Fallan, M. *The Meaning of Educational Change.* New York: Teachers College Press, 1982.

Galloway, C. M., (ed.), "Curriculum Change: Promise and Practice," *Theory into Practice,* Vol. XXII, No. 3, Summer 1983.

Goodlad, J. I. *Dynamics of Educational Change.* New York: McGraw-Hill Co., 1975.

Goodlad, J. I. *A Place Called School.* New York: McGraw-Hill Co., 1984.

Hall, G., and S. Loucks, "Teacher Concerns as a Basis for Facilitating and Personalizing Staff Development," in Lieberman, A., and L. Miller, (eds.). *Staff Development: New Demands, New Realities, New Perspectives.* New York: Teachers College Press, 1979.

Hurn, C. *The Limits and Possibilities of Schooling: An Introduction to the Sociology of Education.* Boston: Allyn and Bacon, 1978.

Lieberman, A., and L. Miller. *Teachers, Their World and Their Work: Implications for School Improvement.* Alexandria, VA: Association for Supervision and Curriculum Development, 1984.

Sarason, S. *The Cultures of the School and the Problem of Change.* Boston: Allyn and Bacon, 1971.

## CHAPTER 3 NOTE

1. J. Mickelson, *Curriculum Theory and Development.* Philadelphia, PA: College of Education, Temple University.

# CHAPTER 4

# Techniques for Planning and Implementing Staff Training

AMONG THE MANY ways in which staff development can be facilitated, training is but one. However, it is one of the most important mechanisms for stimulating change in early childhood settings. Since training participation represents active involvement in learning, it is safe to say that training for early childhood staff should be an ongoing process, but it should never be unplanned or haphazard in occurrence. If any of the wide range of training options are to be utilized, they should be a carefully integrated element of the overall program plan.

In this chapter we will examine the role, planning, and implementation of training to benefit those who work with young children.

## A DEFINITION

It is perhaps best to begin by describing what constitutes training for early childhood staff. Training occurs when by some instructional mechanism (such as lecture or modeling by a trainer-specialist, or use of learning materials, books, films or experiences, and so forth) staff are introduced to new concepts or skills related to their roles in the children's programs.

Training may occur for a variety of reasons: the director may determine that it is needed; staff may request training in accordance with their perceived needs; state or federally funded programs may receive a training mandate; or parents involved in the program can aid in identifying needs.

Training may be accomplished in a variety of ways. Staff may be enrolled in college programs that award credit for participation. The early childhood center may sponsor inservice (in-house) training designed to meet specific needs of the staff. Yet another option is the training that occurs at conferences sponsored by professional organizations. Finally, training can be highly personalized, as when individual staff members pursue their own professional interests. In the next section, we will briefly explore the advantages and disadvantages of each of these avenues for staff training.

## HOW COLLEGE AND UNIVERSITY TRAINING PROGRAMS AFFECT EARLY CHILDHOOD STAFF

In the early 1970s, college-based programs designed to prepare persons for child-care settings were limited. The number of early childhood professionals and scholars was small, and there was great struggle to achieve recognition as a discipline. Since that time, numerous institutions of higher learning have become involved in the process of training early childhood educators. Furthermore, many of those who entered the profession in the early stages when training was not required have opted to return to school to earn one or more of the many certificates or degrees available. Obviously, the early childhood community and individual programs are considerably strengthened by the rise in the numbers of professionally prepared specialists now staffing our programs. We would like to suggest, however, that there are a number of issues to be thought through when considering a college or university program as director-selected training option.

## Advantages of These Training Programs

From the advantage viewpoint, the college program is generally staffed by schooled, experienced persons. Those individuals who provide instructions for the staff are likely to have worked in a variety of programs for young children, conducted research in the field, even written texts and articles dealing with child development topics. In addition, the college environment draws to it a wide array of learners representing various backgrounds, cultural groups, and experiences. This increases opportunities for ancillary learning.

Colleges have a broad range of learning facilities, such as laboratory schools, libraries, and the remedial centers where student learning deficits can be addressed by specialists. For many students, the collegiate atmosphere stimulates interest in subjects that broaden the learning experience and influence individual development positively. When the staff members learn, for example, about art, history, or music, they become potential conveyors of that information to the children.

## Disadvantages of These Training Programs

What is the impact, however, on the early childhood center when the staff are introduced to educational philosophy that is in conflict with that espoused by the director? How does the director respond when the staff begin to ask challenging philosophical questions proposed by their college instructor? How does a director work along with college faculty to assure continuity of learning and continuity between program and goals of college instruction?

These questions do not imply that college courses are an unsatisfactory or troublesome mode of training. Rather we wish to convey the importance of planning and involvement in college training on the part of the early childhood administrator. It is the absence of collaboration that creates a hindrance to the success of university courses as a training mechanism.

There are other potential drawbacks to consider. Since the funding cutbacks, which impacted on training availability for early childhood personnel in federally sponsored programs, many programs have lacked sufficient monies to enable all staff to attend school. As a result, scheduling participation in courses must be done on a staggered basis, with some staff participating in college classes one semester while others wait their turn. Some programs have no such funds available to them, so the staff must pay entirely for their own education. This may be difficult to do on a child-care worker's salary[1] and gives the director no options for input in college program selection.

The same funding cuts that affected training monies made substitute salaries a disappearing budget item. Even if staff manage to pay tuition, the director may not be able to provide coverage that enables daytime class attendance.

These funding problems can be the ingredients for disquiet among staff. Some may wonder why one person received "preferential" treatment. Still others may perceive the evidences of learning demonstrated by the student-staff member as a threat to their own positions and expertise.

High on the list of disadvantages is that completing college courses does not guarantee the growth of competencies. Although the absorption of developmental and learning theory is important, college instruction tends to focus on conceptualization, often at the expense of the corresponding practice skills and activities. In other words, recitation of Piaget's stages of cognitive development is valueless if one cannot identify their characteristics in the youngsters in the classroom and create activities to promote intellectual development.

## IN-HOUSE TRAINING FOR EARLY CHILDHOOD STAFF

Many directors have found that scheduling in-house training is an effective way to address staff development needs. In-house training is that designed exclusively to address the concerns of one program, its participants and personnel. Its advantages are clear cut. Conducted on-site, during hours convenient for staff, everyone can be included in the training process. Planned by the director, the content, methods, and assessment of training effectiveness remain within control of the program's administrator. In-house training is a means to directly address staff development and overall program goals. The director usually has control where the selection of training leaders is concerned, and there is less concern that opposing philosophy or concepts will be presented in the training content.

The main disadvantage of in-house training includes the absence of outside influences (with the exception of a consultant-trainer), which can be the stimulus for different ideas and discussion. Many a center's staff, without outside input, begin to believe that there is no need for change and growth. Individuals, milieu, and program eventually stagnate when such thinking pervades.

## CONFERENCE WORKSHOP TRAINING

Most of the national early childhood organizations, their affiliates, and many of the regional special-interest children's organizations sponsor annual conferences or institutes designed for their membership and public education. Keynote addresses are usually made by major spokespersons in the field or those who influence public policy. Usually such conferences include a series of short lectures, workshops, or panel discussions dealing with topics of specific interest to participants. Although brief (approximately forty-five minutes to two hours in length), these sessions can be invaluable in introducing to or updating professionals on a variety of subjects. Theory, research findings, new programs, and teaching techniques are but a few of the topics covered when professional organizations hold their yearly meetings. Even administrative concerns are addressed.

When the staff of an early childhood program can attend a conference together, there can be many enriching experiences. Membership in a professional organization, which usually comes with payment of the conference fee, helps to foster a sense of professionalism among staff. If small groups of staff attend various sessions, then the next staff meeting can become a forum for sharing and discussing information learned. There are few disadvantages to regular conference attendance, and it is essential for those wishing to keep abreast of developments in the field.

## INDIVIDUAL TRAINING ACTIVITIES

There are many administrators, teachers, and others in the early childhood profession who are interested in development activities. Some have even devised their own plan for professional growth and have set goals to be achieved each year. If a director encounters such persons among program staff, he or she should provide strong encouragement and help those individuals meet their goals. Without this support, many people with potential become discouraged and eventually experience burnout.

It is not enough, however, to be merely a strong supporter of individual efforts to learn. Growing as an early childhood professional involves a process whereby we learn to share, rather than covet, our learning. Directors can help the staff by providing the mechanisms and settings conducive to that sharing. To address this more specifically consider the following:

- *Opportunities for sharing* through settings such as staff projects and meetings, parents and board meetings, and community-involvement activities.

- *Support for sharing* must be verbal. "I would enjoy hearing what you learned in your class this week," accompanied by a warm, encouraging voice and similar facial expression are examples of support mechanisms.
- *Atmosphere for sharing* is attitudinal in nature. The director shares whatever he or she has been learning through course work, reading, and conference attendance, in these ways modeling desired cooperation for others.
- *Rewards for sharing* are frequent and designed to raise the esteem of those who share. "Since Eileen has been reading about parent involvement, perhaps she would like to lead our discussion," is one way of reinforcing individual learning.

Examples of an individual training plan would include university classes, professional reading, visits to other programs and volunteer staff exchanges, subscription to journals and periodicals in the field, membership in professional societies, research studies, and apprenticeship to mentors in the field.

## UTILIZING THE TRAINING OPTION

Terrance Deal and Allen Kennedy, authors of *Corporate Cultures: The Rites and Rituals of Corporate Life*, wrote "Even if people understand and accept a change, they often don't have the required skills and ability to carry out the new plan." Therein, Deal and Kennedy have hit upon the key indicator that training is needed; change is about to occur.[2]

Training may result from a policy, procedural, or funding change. Introduction of new curriculum or teaching methods can be a training motivator (see Chapter 3). As previously mentioned, training may also be required by a funding soure, as the Head Start program is annually mandated to do. But there are other indications that a training program should be undertaken. Staff may point out specific needs, or these may be observed by the director. Parents may make suggestions regarding home-school or staff-child interactions that are stimulators of training. Training may also be a reinforcer of concepts, policies, or procedures. While the staff may be familiar with these, reminders are occasionally needed. Directors must be attuned to those events in the day-to-day functioning of the program that signify training needs.

### Identifying Staff Training Topics

Although early childhood directors make regular observations of staff and hear personnel concerns and parental suggestions, it is not always a simple task to identify the specific source of a problem. Training is most effective when a director has given ample consideration to the overall situation in a center and determined how best to meet specific needs through training activity. Figure 4–1 provides step-by-step procedures for identifying training themes.

## Developing a Training Agenda

Constructing a training plan involves a number of important considerations. The director must identify the most appropriate method of delivery of the training under consideration. Previously, the examples were given of training through college courses, in-house activities, conference workshops, and individual activities. A director might consider available funds, type of center-trainer collaboration and level of input, the setting, as well as other factors when making this decision.

A second factor in the design of the training plan is the development of objectives to be achieved by the training activity. Once the topic has been selected, a statement of objectives must be a priority. The authors have discovered that a great many individuals involved in training design habitually plan training content in advance of objectives. It is the objectives that determine the content, methods, techniques, and how training outcomes will be measured.

Let's take a look at the following examples of a goal and objective of staff development:

- *Goal*—Staff will develop a better understanding of home-school relationships. (NOTE: This is not an aim likely to be achieved by a single training activity. Rather, such a statement might be included in the program's staff development and training plan for the year.)
- *Objective*—Staff will develop a list of five home-school activities designed to improve parent-teacher relationships. (NOTE: This objective meets several essential criteria. First, it can be achieved as a result of one training activity or a short series of activities. Second, the aforementioned "list" of home-school activities provides the means for measuring staff understanding of parent-teacher interactions.)

Developing objectives is a process further complicated by the fact that many people confuse them with goals. Bear in mind that goals are long-term outcomes of program components. Objectives, on the other hand, are short-term and may be written in measurable terms. Figure 4–2 shows a worksheet you can use to see if you know the difference between a goal and an objective.

The third element of the training plan is the determination of training content. It is at this point that the complete range of information to be included in training sessions would be specified. Although this task would be somewhat more difficult if a college course were to be the training avenue than it would be for planning in-house training, the content-determination process is still an important step. It suggests the importance of matching training needs with course descriptions.

## CHECKLIST FOR IDENTIFYING STAFF TRAINING THEMES

Follow these guidelines to identify the training topics most appropriate for your early childhood staff:

____1. Identify major training areas as you see them. These will be the overall categories from which the topics for training will be chosen. Examples of these larger areas would be child development, curriculum development, environmental planning, interpersonal skills. Making this selection and pinpointing the subtopics in each category provides structure and organization for the identification process.

> Example: Curriculum Development (training area)
> (subtopics) 1. determining children's developmental needs
> 2. unit plan development
> 3. evaluating lessons and activities
> 4. selecting materials to implement lessons

____2. Gather baseline data regarding training needs. This should be accomplished in several different ways.

a. *Director Observations:* Use some competency-derived observation tool. Guidelines based upon the Child Development Associate competencies and functional areas may be useful. (See *Skills for Preschool Teachers,* second edition, by J. J. Beaty). Do not forget to observe outdoors, as well as in the office and support-service areas. Support staff are as critical to program success as teachers and caregivers.

b. *Staff Feedback:* May be gathered in a number of ways. A formal technique involves the utilization of an information-gathering device, such as a needs form to be completed by staff. Additionally, staff input can be gleaned through suggestion boxes and one-to-one director-staff conferences. (See Chapter 1 for Training Needs Form.)

c. *Parent, Policy Board, and Community Input:* The suggestion box can be utilized for this purpose as well. In addition, parent meetings and individual conferences are excellent opportunities for home-to-school input regarding program, personnel, and policies.

d. *Director Self-Evaluation:* Examination of the administrator's role in relation to staff can be a useful way of determining where the daily input of the director might benefit from the reinforcement provided by training.

____3. Review program goals to establish the correlation between these and apparent training needs. Training should be geared toward the overall aims of the program.

____4. Narrow down the possibilities. Remember not all training needs can or should be addressed simultaneously. The best way to achieve the narrowing-down process is to prioritize. That is, identify pressing problems that should be addressed by training first, second, third, and so forth.

© 1987 by The Center for Applied Research in Education, Inc.

**FIGURE 4–1**

____5. Talk over your findings with staff. While it is not essential that a director have staff approval to plan a training program, their concurrence and support can be useful and may help to secure the success of training.

____6. Identify the basic content to be included in training sessions. This involves writing a broad description of the information and ideas to be conveyed to staff.

____7. Develop specific objectives for training. These might describe specific skills staff are to develop as a result of training.

____8. Specify the environment and techniques to be used in training, that is, what setting and instructional strategies will be most likely to achieve the stated objectives. At what levels will participants be involved in training?

____9. Schedule the date and time of training. Consider the work schedules and personal situations of those staff to be involved.

____10. Identify a training leader. Work with that individual to assure that objectives will be met and suitable training techniques utilized.

____11. Review the training agenda with staff. Utilize motivators to promote staff interest and involvement in activities.

____12. Along with training participants evaluate the results of training and determine future staff development activities.

**FIGURE 4–1 cont'd.**

## IS IT A GOAL OR AN OBJECTIVE?

*Directions:* Read the items below carefully. *Remember the characteristics of an objective.* Then decide whether each of the statements is an OBJECTIVE or a GOAL. If the statement is an "objective" place an *O* in the space provided. If the statement is a "goal" place a *G* in the space provided.

____ 1. The child will be able to count from one to five when shown a group of five triangles and asked, "How many triangles are in this row?"

____ 2. The program will provide opportunities for children to develop the skills of observation.

____ 3. Given a picture showing five different community helpers, the child will be able to tell which person is the fireman, which is the mailman, etc.

____ 4. The child will be able to tell whether a truck is "on" or "under" the table when the truck is placed there by the teacher and the child is asked, "Where is the toy truck?"

____ 5. The program will provide opportunities for the development of large muscles.

____ 6. The child will be able to hop on one foot.

____ 7. The program will provide opportunities for children to develop personal hygiene skills.

____ 8. The child will be able to cross the street safely.

____ 9. When shown pictures of faces showing different emotions, the child will be able to tell which face is "sad."

____10. The child will be able to identify the letter his or her name begins with, when he or she is shown the letters H, M, T, and A and told, "Please point to the first letter in your name."

____11. During lunch time the child will be able to hold his or her fork correctly.

____12. The child will be able to write the letter of his or her last name.

____13. The program will expose children to various art forms.

____14. The child will be able to pour milk from the small pitcher to the glass when asked to serve milk to another child.

____15. The program will help to develop the cognitive skill of classification.

**FIGURE 4–2**

Once content has been identified, training techniques can be selected (if sessions are to take place in-house). The environment for training, types of participant activities, and instructional methods are some of the technical considerations. These are addressed in detail in Chapter 5.

The fifth consideration is the timing of training. At certain times of the year, or at certain points in the day, staff are more available and receptive to training. For example, summer is vacation time for many people. Often personnel are more receptive to training when it occurs in the early fall, at the onset of the school year. By the same token, training should be avoided just prior to weekends and holidays. No one preparing for Thanksgiving wants to focus on work-related issues. Even time of day is a factor. Staff should not be asked to relinquish their break time or to stay for training at the end of a long work day. Whenever possible, training should be scheduled for days set aside for this purpose, when children are out of the building on holiday or when substitute coverage can be scheduled.

Finally, evaluation tools must be identified. When a consultant-trainer is utilized, that individual generally has input into the assessment process. We strongly suggest, however, that whatever tools are utilized to measure training, outcomes should include the criteria for skills- or knowledge-mastery activities. (See Chapter 11 for specific suggestions on evaluation.)

## Selecting Training Leaders

The choice of a training leader is one equal in importance to the selection of topics. While Chapters 2 and 6 deal with aspects of this process, there are several qualifications that should be introduced or reiterated here.

- *Areas of expertise*—individuals are more experienced or learned in one area than another. A trainer should be selected on the basis of knowledge of the training topic.

- *Rapport with staff*—may be actual or assumed. That is, it may be known that a trainer has the interpersonal skills needed to effectively communicate with participants, or essential skills may be assumed on the basis of the trainer's experience or reputation.

- *Previous training experience*—is an important determinant because knowledge of training techniques is not innate and is separate from topic expertise. One can be informed about the topic, but be a poor trainer.

- *Understanding of learning styles*—a trainer must be open to the questions, body language and other indications from trainees that learning is or is not occurring.

A trainer may be the program director, a college faculty member, an employed consultant, or even a staff member from the center. Regardless of who is selected, the critical issue is the individual's ability to effectively convey information so that all staff may benefit.

## Selecting Staff for Training

There are, unfortunately, times when not all staff have the option of participating in training. It may be determined that not everyone on the staff requires the training in question. In these circumstances, the strong interpersonal skills of the director are called upon to identify training participants without bruising egos and hurting feelings. Those selected may feel either pleased or "picked on." Those not chosen may feel slighted or anxious. There are no absolute techniques for handling these situations, but sensitivity and other staff development options can go a long way toward maintaining harmonious relations.

When the determining factor in staff selection for training is funding or substitute coverage, choices may be made on the basis of interest. If many staff members express interest in training, choice by lottery is another option. Personnel must be informed about the selection criteria. If all have a sense that they are being treated fairly and other learning opportunities are provided, then most staff will have a positive response to training.

If some staff must be singled out for training participation, a resentful or fearful response alone may interfere and create an attitude not conducive to learning. The director must calm, reassure, and support the staff members who have special learning needs.

## Monitoring Staff Involvement in Training Programs

Whatever the mode of training selected, the director must stay abreast of the information presented and the progress of individual staff members. While it may be possible for administrators to participate along with the staff in some forms of training (such as that occurring in-house), administrators cannot oversee all training activities directly. Nonetheless, it must be assured that training meets objectives, occurs on schedule, and conveys information compatible with early childhood program philosophy.

Some of the ways to monitor the progress of training have been briefly touched upon. Having staff share information with co-workers, parents, and community is one technique for achieving this end. Encouraging staff projects requiring interaction and collaboration is yet another mechanism. The staff may be asked to develop and implement ideas to meet program needs, utilizing newly learned skills and information. The director may conduct assessment observations to determine the skills growth that has occurred to date. Whatever the means, monitoring staff training activities makes it possible for training to remain on target and achieve desired results.

## Beginning the Training Process

When all the planning has been completed, the trainer selected, and the meeting times and places arranged, it is important to stimulate staff interest in forthcoming training events. It is not enough to announce that training has been scheduled and await its beginning. Much in the same way classroom teachers prepare children for field trips with discussion and special activities, directors must work to motivate staff energy and enthusiasm for training. Unfortunately, in many school and business systems, training opportunities are treated in such an uninspired fashion that they become an escape from the work setting. Rather than stimulating professionalism, energy flow, and a sense of challenge, staff development programs can become activities without purpose or reward.

The following are examples of motivators aimed at promoting the success of staff-development activities:

1. Tell an inspirational story about someone in the profession who used learning or educational opportunities as a means to overcome odds and achieve success in the field.

2. Have a fund-raising white elephant, flea market, or bake sale to enable staff to do something special with newly learned skills, for example, redecorate the classroom following an upcoming "Environmental Design Workshop."

3. Find funds in the center budget to pay for a membership or subscribe to a professional journal for all of those completing a course.

4. Give free reign for staff to plan a family day or other parent-child activity.

5. Schedule exchange-observation days at nearby centers in cooperation with directors of other programs.

6. Plan training activities with two or three centers participating together.

7. Announce that hand-lettered certificates will be awarded to each member of the staff who completes training. Post the names of certificate winners where parents and others arriving at the center will see them.

8. Have a short discussion during staff meeting about the expected impact of training on next year's program, for example, adding an infant-toddler classroom will now be possible.

9. Print the list of names of staff involved in training in the center newsletter or in the community newspaper.

10. Have teachers send home requests for curriculum materials prior to a scheduled training activity: baby food jars, dry macaroni, old magazines, and so forth, that will be used in the classroom after a training session in "Creative Expression."

## RECOMMENDED READING

Beaty, J. J. *Skills for Preschool Teachers*, Second Edition. Columbus, OH: Charles E. Merrill Publishing Co., 1984.

Diamondstone, J. *Designing, Leading and Evaluating Workshops for Teachers and Parents: A Manual for Trainers and Leadership Personnel in Early Childhood Education*. Ypsilanti, MI: High/Scope Press, 1980.

Donaldson, L., and E. Scannel. *Human Resource Development: The New Trainer's Guide*. Reading, MA: Addison-Wesley, 1978.

Hildebrand, V. *Management of Child Development Centers*. New York: Macmillan Publishing Company, 1984.

Hines, R. "Techniques for Preparing People to Work with Young Children," in *Illinois Teacher*, Vol. 26, No. 5, May/June 1983, pp. 186–187.

Honig, A. S., and J. Lally. *Infant Caregiving: A Design for Training*. Syracuse, NY: Syracuse University Press, 1981.

*Improving School Staffs: An Administrator's Guide to Staff Development*, Volume III, AASA Executive Handbook Series. Arlington, VA: American Association of School Administrators, 1974.

Jones, L., et al. *The Child Development Associate Program: A Guide to Program Administration*. Washington, D.C.: U.S. Department of Health and Human Services, Offices of Human Development Services, 1981.

McFadden, D. M. (ed.). *Early Childhood Development Programs and Services: Planning for Action*. Washington, D.C.: National Association for the Education of Young Children, 1972.

McGreal, L. *Successful Teacher Evaluation*. Alexandria, VA: Association for Supervision and Curriculum Development, 1983.

Rothenberg, D. (comp.). *Directory of Education Programs for Adults Who Work with Young Children*. Washington, D.C.: National Association for the Education of Young Children, 1979.

Zumwalt, K. K. *Improving Teaching*. Alexandria, VA: Association for Supervision and Curriculum Development, 1983.

## CHAPTER 4 NOTES

1. R. Rupp and J. Travers, "James Faces Day Care: Perspectives on Quality and Cost," in eds. E. Zigler and E. Gordon, *Day Care: Scientific and Social Policy Issues*. Boston: Auburn House, 1982, pp. 88–89.

2. T. E. Deal and A. A. Kennedy, *Corporate Cultures: The Rites and Rituals of Corporate Life*. Reading, MA: Addison-Wesley Publishing Company, Inc., 1982, p. 165.

# CHAPTER 5

# Materials and Resources for Staff Training

EACH TRAINING tool used by staff developers conveys information in a different fashion. Each has a different impact on the learner. In some cases the impact is entirely intellectual. But training resources can also have sensory development consequences. That is, training resources can provide auditory, visual, tactile, even olfactory information to learners. It is for these reasons that training materials and resources should be considered a worthwhile part of the staff development process, for when trainers appeal to a wide range of learning modalities, they are most likely to find the avenues leading to cognition and skills mastery. Individuals learn in a wide variety of ways. While some can easily absorb and utilize lecture-given information, others benefit from hands-on or visual experiences. The role of the trainer is to reach and teach as many learners as possible.

## TRAINING MATERIALS

Occasionally, a trainer is such a charismatic individual, such an excellent speaker, that no props, resources, or teaching aids are necessary in order to convey information to learners. But most of us are not so talented. From another viewpoint, using materials and other training resources can be a valuable assist to those involved in staff development. If they are carefully selected for their interest and ability to convey relevant information, these aids can become a trainer's partner. This chapter will look at the many written, audio, visual, and participant involvement activities that can be mobilized by early childhood trainers.

### Written Instruction

Written materials serve two main purposes. They may be a primary training mechanism, as when programmed learning packages are utilized; or written materials may support the lecture or discussion component of training. Handouts, books, charts and graphs, and written exercises are examples of these.

### Books

Books may be used by trainers in a variety of ways. Training that occurs in the college classroom may employ assigned reading to stimulate discussion or lay the groundwork for instructor lecture. Other methods of training may utilize books as resources during or following training. Books or bibliographies related to a training topic can be provided in order to illustrate for participants some of the means to follow up on or obtain additional information.

For example, the following is a selected bibliography of readings on classroom and behavior management for teachers of young children:

## READINGS IN CLASSROOM AND BEHAVIOR MANAGEMENT

Axelrod, S. *Behavior Modification for the Classroom Teacher,* Second Edition. New York: McGraw-Hill Book Co., 1983.

Canfield, J., and H. C. Wells. *100 Ways to Enhance Self-Concept in the Classroom: A Handbook for Teachers and Parents.* Englewood Cliffs, NJ: Prentice Hall, 1976.

Charles, C. M. *Building Classroom Discipline: From Models to Practice.* New York: Longman, Inc., 1981.

*Discipline in the Classroom,* Revised Edition. Washington, D.C.: National Education Association, 1974.

Dobson, J. *Dare to Discipline.* New York: Bantam Books, 1977.

Duke, D. L. *Helping Teachers Manage Classrooms.* Washington, D.C.: Association for Supervision and Curriculum Development, 1982.

Eglash, A. *Please Don't Step on My Castle: A Passive Attack Upon Assertive Discipline.* St. Luis Obispo, CA: Quest Press, 1981.

*Free to Be...You and Me.* New York: McGraw-Hill Book Co., 1975. (Includes film, filmstrips, cassettes, posters, book, games.)

Hymes, J. L. *Behavior and Misbehavior: A Teacher's Guide to Action.* Englewood Cliffs, NJ: Prentice-Hall, Inc., 1955.

Kerr, M. M., and C. M. Nelson. *Strategies for Managing Behavior Problems in the Classroom.* Columbus, OH: Charles E. Merrill Publishing Co., 1983.

Leatzow, N., C. Neuhauser, and L. Wilmes. *Creating Discipline in the Early Childhood Classroom.* Provo, UT: Brigham Young University Press, 1983.

Lemlech, J. K. *Classroom Management.* New York: Harper and Row, Publishers, 1979.

Silberman, M. L., and S. A. Wheelan. *How to Discipline Without Feeling Guilty: Assertive Relationships with Children.* New York: Hawthorn Books, 1980.

Tanner, L. N. *Classroom Discipline for Effective Teaching and Learning.* New York: Holt, Rinehart and Winston, 1978.

Wlodkowski, R. J. *Discipline and Motivation: A Genuine Partnership* (cassette). Washington, DC: National Education Association, 1978.

## Charts and Graphs

These materials may be utilized to record information gathered by trainees. For example, during an in-house workshop on classroom management skills, caregivers at Grant Child Development Center were asked to observe some children for a 15-minute period to look for situations that were the precursors of behavior problems (see Figure 5–1). When the caregivers returned to their training group, the gathered data was recorded on a chart. This became the basis for discussion in the training group about techniques for promoting positive behavior in young children.

**SAMPLE PARTICIPATION CHART FOR RECORDING
OBSERVED INFORMATION**

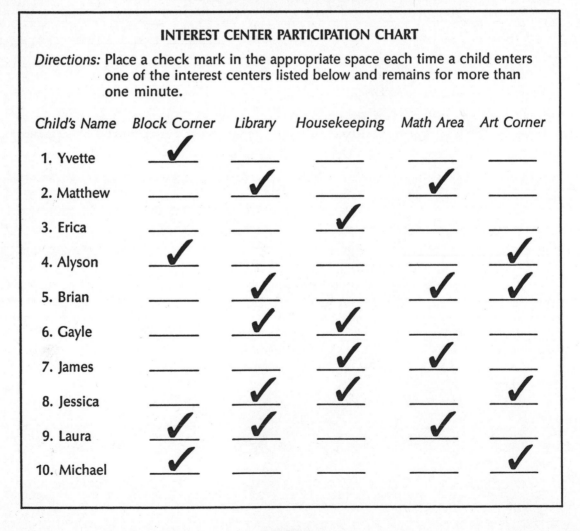

**INTEREST CENTER PARTICIPATION CHART**

*Directions:* Place a check mark in the appropriate space each time a child enters one of the interest centers listed below and remains for more than one minute.

| Child's Name | Block Corner | Library | Housekeeping | Math Area | Art Corner |
|---|---|---|---|---|---|
| 1. Yvette | ✓ | | | | |
| 2. Matthew | | ✓ | | ✓ | |
| 3. Erica | | | ✓ | | |
| 4. Alyson | ✓ | | | | ✓ |
| 5. Brian | | ✓ | | ✓ | ✓ |
| 6. Gayle | | ✓ | ✓ | | |
| 7. James | | | ✓ | ✓ | |
| 8. Jessica | | ✓ | ✓ | | ✓ |
| 9. Laura | ✓ | ✓ | | ✓ | |
| 10. Michael | ✓ | | | | ✓ |

**FIGURE 5–1**

Graphs may also be used to record information, or they may serve to present data, such as that collected through research (see Figure 5–2).

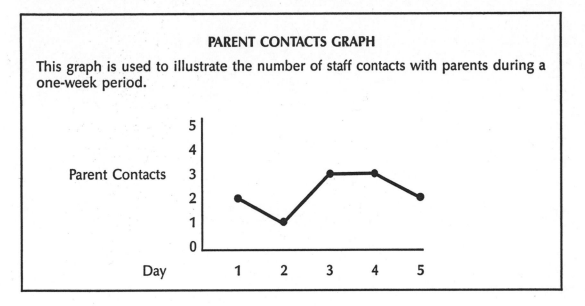

**PARENT CONTACTS GRAPH**

This graph is used to illustrate the number of staff contacts with parents during a one-week period.

**FIGURE 5–2**

## Handouts

Handouts are probably the most widely used technique for reinforcing training information. They are generally some form of reiteration of the trainer's presentation. One of the most helpful aspects of handouts is their use for future reference. If one of the training objectives is to teach participants to follow certain procedures, handouts can stimulate questions during training and refresh the memory later. Figure 5–3 shows a sample handout that could be distributed as a follow-up activity to a workshop on parent involvement. Figure 5–4 is another sample training handout giving suggestions for promoting positive behavior in young children.

NOTE: Trainers should be cautious not to overuse or rely too heavily on handouts to provide information.

## Programmed Learning Materials

These materials are actually a training method rather than just a set of materials. They are usually a highly individualized, self-paced mode of conveying information. Learners receive informational packets, which they read and on which they are later quizzed regarding the contents. Programmed learning materials generally contain the means for trainees to self-check their work. The trainer acts in more of a facilitative, resource role when these materials are utilized. Figure 5–5 gives an example of a programmed learning

## FACTORS THAT INTERFERE WITH PARENT INVOLVEMENT

_____ 1. Parent's own unhappy school experiences.

_____ 2. Parent's previous experience with other schools or teachers.

_____ 3. Parent's concern that his/her language or clothing may be inappropriate for appearance at school.

_____ 4. Teacher's use of difficult-to-understand academic jargon.

_____ 5. School's perpetuation of hands-off-education attitude toward parents.

_____ 6. Parent's preconceived notion (derived from teacher or school) of what roles and which activities constitute involvement.

_____ 7. Family problems, including physical and mental illness, handicapping conditions, child or spouse abuse, drug or alcohol abuse.

_____ 8. Parent's lack of comfort to express own needs or needs of child.

_____ 9. Parent's belief that teachers are the authority on childhood education.

_____ 10. Lack of familiarity by parents of rights with regard to child, access to school records, etc.

_____ 11. Parent's preconceived ideas about other families, their lifestyle, financial status.

_____ 12. Inaccessibility or inconvenience of parent involvement activities for some families.

_____ 13. Impression given by "overactive" parents that involvement by others is unwelcome.

_____ 14. Competition between parents and teachers for knowledge and affection by child.

_____ 15. Failure of school to tie involvement activities into system of parental belief, cultural values, and motivations.

**FIGURE 5–3**

# SUGGESTIONS FOR PROMOTING POSITIVE BEHAVIOR IN YOUNG CHILDREN

_____ 1. Recognize developmental changes as they occur in young children and expect the emergence of new behaviors.

_____ 2. Reduce situations and remove objects known to cause or create fears in children.

_____ 3. Give children names for their emotions and provide and demonstrate appropriate ways to express those feelings.

_____ 4. Recognize the urgency of the young child's needs for rest, food, and comfort, and recognize the various ways in which those needs are expressed.

_____ 5. Avoid overstimulating or overtiring children and expecting them to make a quick adjustment to another mood or level of activity.

_____ 6. Provide daily one-to-one interaction with every child.

_____ 7. Permit age-appropriate choices and child-to-adult feedback.

_____ 8. Make both expectations and consequences for misbehavior clear, and follow rules yourself.

_____ 9. Be consistent regarding both rules and enforcement of discipline.

_____ 10. Avoid pushing children into stressful or fear-producing situations.

_____ 11. Provide children with responsibilities at an ever-challenging level.

_____ 12. Provide frequent reinforcement for appropriate, cooperative behavior.

_____ 13. Arrange for many types and levels of activity during the day, such as "active" and "quiet," "messy" and "neat."

_____ 14. Give children time to practice responding appropriately to adult expectations.

_____ 15. Respect children's belongings, family life, and privacy.

**FIGURE 5–4**

**CHILD DEVELOPMENT ASSOCIATE TRAINING PROGRAM***
(Sample Programmed Materials)
Unit I
Module 4
11 Basic Concepts

*Purpose of Activity:* To review essential material related to much of what we have read, observed, heard, and know.

*Directions for Activity 11:*

1. Read the information contained in your reading material folder entitled "Basic Concept for Nutrition Education."

2. Most of these you have read in another format or heard before.

3. This is similar to a final review.

4. When you have finished your reading put it aside and use the activity sheet 11. Read the instructions before you begin.

5. When you have finished, check your answers in your reading materials.


**Activity Sheet 11**

Please draw a line to the correct answers.

Nutrition —the nutrients in food and food sources

—the food we eat and how the body uses it

—the exact amounts of food we eat

Every food has —the required nutrients

—some nutritional value

—energy-supplying nutrients

Nutrients —are required only of children

—are required only of adults

—are required by all persons

A balanced diet —can be obtained from different foods

—can be obtained from a combination of many foods

—is necessary only for the aged

Check your answers with the information contained in the "Basic Concepts for Nutrition Education."

*This material taken from *The Child Development Associate Training Program,* Unit I, Module 4, T. H. Stern (ed.). Philadelphia: Research for Better Schools, 1974, pp. 29–32. Reprinted by permission.

**FIGURE 5–5**

*Basic Concepts for Nutrition Education*

1. Nutrition is the food you eat and how the body uses it.
   —We eat food to live, grow, keep healthy and well, and to get energy for work and play.

2. Food is made up of different nutrients needed for growth and health.
   —All nutrients needed by the body are available through food.
   —Many kinds and combinations of food can lead to a well-balanced diet.
   —No food, by itself, has all the nutrients for full growth and health.
   —Each nutrient has specific uses in the body.
   —Most nutrients do their best work in the body when teamed with other nutrients.

3. All persons, throughout life, have need for the same nutrients, but in varying amounts.
   —The amounts of nutrients needed are influenced by age, sex, size, activity, and state of health.
   —Suggestions for the kinds and amounts of food needed are made by trained scientists.

4. The way food is handled influences the amount of nutrients in food, its safety, appearance, and taste.
   —Handling means everything that happens to food while it is being grown, processed, stored, and prepared for eating.

*Points of Emphasis for Food Handling*

1. Points of emphasis
   —Sanitation—one of the most important aspects of a feeding program. Carelessness can cause the spread of disease with drastic consequences.

2. Good sanitation practices are just as important as feeding children nutritious, body-building meals.
   —Clean hands, utensils and equipment
   —Clean and healthy workers
   —Good food-handling practices

3. Methods used to prevent disease and other drastic consequences (roaches, rodent infestations)
   —All personnel should meet health standards set by local and state health authorities.
   —Persons with infected cuts, sores, colds, or other diseases do not serve or prepare food.
   —All hands are washed before serving, handling, and eating.
   —All drinking utensils are properly handled and not shared.
   —Inspections are made by local health agency authorities.
   —Examination of food is done when delivered for spoilage or contamination.
   —Protection of foods from infestation.
   —All fruits and vegetables served raw should be washed before serving.
   —Discard portions of food served but not eaten.
   —All appliances and equipment should be kept in good working order.

**FIGURE 5–5 cont'd.**

module on child nutrition. Note that it contains basic nutritional concepts and a post-test measure of trainee understanding of the materials. When one of the authors was director of the Child Development Associate Training Program that utilized these materials, programmed learning was used in concert with lecture, demonstration, field experience, and audio-visual materials in order to address a range of learning styles.

## Written Exercises

Written exercises are often used by trainers to enable participants to self-check their understanding of new information. These exercises follow a lecture, demonstration, or film presentation and are most beneficial when the completed exercises are discussed by the trainer and participants. Figure 5–6 shows a sample training follow-up activity, and Figure 5–7 shows a sample training activity.

## AUDIO-VISUAL PRESENTATIONS

For many years, training resources were limited to garbled audio tapes and scratched or blurry films. Today the quality and range of audio-visual resources has improved enormously. There are many audio-visual aids available to staff trainers and program directors through film-lending libraries, distribution groups, professional organizations (which often offer discounted merchandise to members), and public broadcasting groups. Slides, videotapes, and other audio-visual tools can greatly enhance the impact of training, creating an auditory and/or visual image of the concepts or issues being discussed. It is well worth the time and energy of any staff developer/trainer to explore the potential role of audio visuals in the training program.

## Audio Tapes

These are available from many educational and mental-health organizations. They are usually lecturers or keynote addresses given by experts or major spokespersons in the field. Audio-tape presentations should be followed by trainer-led discussion of the theory or concepts presented by the speaker. From an equipment standpoint, only a tape recorder is required.

## Films

In recent years there have been a number of excellent films produced related to child development, early childhood education and child-care topics (see Chapter 12). Many of these are available for rental from the companies that

## RATE YOUR PARENT INVOLVEMENT POTENTIAL

*Directions:* Mark each statement True or False.

|  | True | False |
|---|---|---|
| 1. I regularly use the suggestions and ideas contributed by parents. | _____ | _____ |
| 2. I feel tense when parents enter my classroom/office. | _____ | _____ |
| 3. I contact parents when a child does well in school. | _____ | _____ |
| 4. I feel that some parents have abdicated parental responsibilities. | _____ | _____ |
| 5. I accept differences in lifestyle and child-rearing attitudes among parents. | _____ | _____ |
| 6. I believe that parents do not understand or appreciate how difficult an educator's work is. | _____ | _____ |
| 7. I feel that many parents are not interested in their children. | _____ | _____ |
| 8. I encourage parents to drop in to school unannounced. | _____ | _____ |
| 9. I believe that parents who let their children come to school in inappropriate clothing are irresponsible. | _____ | _____ |
| 10. I believe that children's school problems are usually indicative of poor quality family life | _____ | _____ |

**FIGURE 5–6**

## LABEL OR BEHAVIOR QUIZ

*Instructions:* Place a check next to those statements that pinpoint behavior. Do not mark those that label children.

_____ 1. Lewis loves buttermilk.

_____ 2. Andy painted several pictures today.

_____ 3. Marci bites her fingernails.

_____ 4. Paula threw another temper tantrum.

_____ 5. Alice is a nervous child.

_____ 6. Martin often hits and kicks his brother.

_____ 7. Allan is very cooperative in the classroom.

_____ 8. Mary Ellen is withdrawn.

_____ 9. Russell frequently interrupts when others are talking.

_____ 10. Lois seems to be a bright child.

*Instructions:* Choose between the two statements. Select the one that describes a child's behavior.

_____ A. Ann's mother describes her as an insecure child.

_____ B. Ann's mother says that Ann always cries when left with someone else.

_____ A. Michael often hugs his teacher when he arrives at school.

_____ B. Michael is a very affectionate child.

_____ A. Lois seems to be a bright child.

_____ B. Lois recognizes all her letters and numbers.

_____ A. Ruth always says, "No!" when asked to help pick up toys.

_____ B. Ruth is very uncooperative.

**FIGURE 5–7**

distribute them. Longer in length than slide/tape presentations, they usually contain more information and cover more issues. A projector and screen (or blank, light-colored wall) are needed for viewing. One drawback of the older projection equipment used by many schools is its tendency to break down at inappropriate times. In addition, older machines lack the self-threading devices that greatly simplify the film loading process.

## Slides and Tapes

These presentations are usually a brief look at some issue or topic in the field. Slides are advantageous if a trainer would like participants to study some aspects of the photographs used. For example, the authors have frequently used a slide/tape presentation of home hazards to illustrate the process of child-proofing one's home or center. Trainees can observe the slides of kitchen, bathroom, and classroom to identify the safety hazards present in each scene. Slide/tape equipment has been considerably simplified by small, compact machines that provide the screen, projector, and tape recorder in one portable case. This is an excellent way of making slide/tape presentations to small groups.

## Videotapes

Videotapes are the newest, widely available mode of viewing training films. With the advent of the video store, many tapes can be rented overnight for a modest sum, and even the tape playback equipment can be inexpensively rented. Although the full range of available videotapes on early childhood cannot be found in the video store at present, many may be rented through film production/distribution groups. Watch for a big increase in the numbers of how-to, self-help tapes in the local video store, as these will soon include more child development and family-issues tapes that can be used for training purposes.

## PARTICIPANT-INVOLVEMENT ACTIVITIES

Many learners appreciate and greatly benefit from the opportunity for active involvement or hands-on participation in training. It is tiring to sit listening to a lecture or watching a film without a chance to comment on the information received. Without regularly spaced opportunities for trainee input, some critical questions are never posed, and useful observations are never heard by the group. There is a broad range of participant-involvement activities, from the simple and easily orchestrated to the complex requiring outside resources. Regardless of their degree of complexity, the benefits of these activities are clear cut. Trainees are able to make a contribution to the proceedings and receive immediate feedback or reward for their participation.

## Group Discussion

Group discussion is the easiest to adapt to the complete range of training programs. Questions or issues may be raised by the trainer or the participants, with the former acting in a facilitating role. There are drawbacks, however. Group discussion is most effective in the small group setting. Often trainees have had little or no experience speaking in a group, and their shyness inhibits participation in short-term training. It takes sensitivity to participant needs and feelings to stimulate a high rate of trainee involvement in discussion.

## Group Games

These were popularized during the 1960s and 1970s when the focus was on getting in touch with oneself and others and the honest expression of emotions. Today, the group-games process is a somewhat controversial participant-involvement tool. One drawback is that it forces trainee involvement, even when not everyone may be ready to participate. Group games may also call for trainees to reveal strengths and weaknesses or personal sides-of-self that they may prefer to keep hidden from colleagues. Many group games should not be attempted unless staff are a tightly knit, cohesive group, willing to be completely open and accepting of one another.

## Observation of Other Programs

Observing other programs is a highly recommended training device. If two or three early childhood programs collaborate on their training plans, sessions can be scheduled at each of the various locations, and observations can be written directly into the training agenda. If this type of rotation training is not possible, observations can be utilized as an assignment between sessions or might be a strongly recommended follow-up activity to training. See Figure 5–8 for an observation form that staff developers can use to generate discussion in a post-visit training session. Of course, an observation form may be designed to look for specific features of the program observed.

## Small-Group Activities

These are another useful way of reinforcing concepts or skills. Unlike the written exercises usually done individually, small-group activities provide support for the shy or hesitant members of the staff. Activities can be done in groups of two to five persons, depending upon overall group size. They are especially effective when a class or training group has been too large for intimate discussion and interactions. The trainer should recommend that each group appoint a recorder and spokesperson to report back to the entire gathering. Figures 5–9 and 5–10 are taken from one of the authors' training

**FIELD TRIP OBSERVATION FORM**

Name:_____

Date:_____

Center/School Visited:_____

Name of Teacher:_____

*Directions:* To the best of your ability answer the following questions and be prepared to discuss them with your training group.

1. List some of the kinds of activities you observed in the classroom (such as free choice, block play, circle, etc.).



2. List the equipment and materials observed in the classroom.



3. How many children are in the classroom?_____

4. How many teachers are in the classroom?_____

5. Are there any parent volunteers working in the classroom?_____
   If so, how many?_____ In what ways are parents participating? _____
   _____

6. Describe any interest centers in the classroom (such as doll corner, library corner, etc.). Use the back of this page if additional space is needed.



7. What features of the classroom did you particularly like? Dislike?



8. Have you observed anything in the classroom that is new to you? If so, please describe what you have seen.

**FIGURE 5–8**

9. List at least one (1) thing you have observed in each of the following areas. You may list an example of a lesson or activity you observed or you may list some things the teacher said to a child/children in each of these areas.

a. Mathematics—

b. Language Arts—

c. Science—

d. Social Studies—

10. How would you describe the interactions of the staff in this program/classroom? Did you observe a team approach being used?

11. Describe any outdoor equipment you see.

12. Describe the use of this equipment by the children.

13. Did you observe any additional outdoor activities, including those conducted by the staff? If so, please describe these.

**FIGURE 5–8 cont'd.**

sessions focusing on the uses of "Observation to Individualize Curriculum for Young Children." Figure 5–9 illustrates a four-phase curriculum individualization plan described to trainees, while 5–10 is a small-group activity completed by persons who practice utilizing the plan.

---

**FOUR-PHASE PLAN FOR INDIVIDUALIZING PROGRAMS FOR YOUNG CHILDREN**

After identifying the skill, concept, or behavior to be developed by the child, and after identifying a series of activities designed to reach the stated goal and the order in which the child should be introduced to them, use the following four-phase plan to help achieve success:

*Phase One:* Conduct a one-to-one, teacher-child lesson to introduce the skill.

*Phase Two:* Select a second activity and pair the child with another who needs practice, or who has mastered the skill. This child-child activity provides repetition or peer tutoring where helpful.

*Phase Three:* Assign the child to an activity, such as a special job or classroom chore to be done alone. This related activity provides opportunity for additional practice and builds the child's confidence in his or her ability to be successful at a newly learned skill.

*Phase Four:* Give the child an opportunity to participate in a skill-related large-group activity. Make certain this is a pressure-free situation. The child will have an opportunity to demonstrate skill mastery and will experience enhanced self-esteem.

NOTE: With the growth of certain skills, especially those related to socialization, much more one-to-one and small-group practice may be needed by the child before becoming involved in a large-group activity.

---

**FIGURE 5–9**

## OTHER TRAINING RESOURCES

Not all training tools are written, audio-visual, or participatory in nature. Staff developers learn to explore resources throughout the early childhood field, those in the community, and those available in the training environment. The final section of this chapter is devoted to identifying and utilizing these additional ways of achieving staff development goals.

### The Training Environment as Resource

The atmosphere in which training occurs is an influential factor often overlooked by training specialists. Atmosphere has several ingredients. The lighting in a room, the room's temperature, and the human interactions are components of the training atmosphere. The setting may also be conducive to

## SMALL GROUP ACTIVITY

Develop a "four-phase plan" to meet the needs of the child described below:

John is five years old. He is taller and heavier than the other children in his preschool class. John seems to be less well-coordinated than other children his age. He often stumbles, bumps into things, and falls. When he goes outdoors, John tends to watch from the sidelines as other children play. He used to join in running games and other activities, but he had many accidents and other children made fun of him. You already know that John has no physical impairments or visual or hearing problems. What plan can you develop to help John?

_____

_____

_____

_____

_____

_____

_____

_____

_____

_____

_____

_____

_____

**FIGURE 5–10**

training when seating, writing, and group-interaction space is comfortable to all involved. Poor lighting produces eye strain. Rooms that are too warm or cold produce a different sort of discomfort in trainees. Trainers are sometimes insensitive to the fact that their constant activity level keeps them warm (in colder weather), while nonparticipatory trainees may feel cold, drowsy, or bored. Seating should be comfortable, depending upon the length of time participants must remain seated. Long sessions should be punctuated with regular breaks. If writing is required, a firm surface should be provided. If a group game or activity is planned, ample space should be allotted for these without the necessity of lifting or moving heavy furniture.

Trainers should estimate space and environmental needs prior to training, plan accordingly, and make adjustments where needed. Next to the training leader, it is the environment that sets the tone for training and contributes significantly to its success or failure.

## RESOURCES IN THE PROFESSION AND COMMUNITY

This section of this chapter deals with the human resources available from among a trainer's colleagues and associates in the field. These are an often overlooked source of information, materials, ideas, and even training itself.

SAMPLE: *Using Training Resources (Professional)*
When Patty R. was the teacher/director of a parent cooperative nursery school, she operated the program on a minuscule budget. As the only teacher, also responsible for planning, implementing, and evaluating the program, Patty was aware of numerous problems. Her co-workers were the children's parents, who worked weekly on a rotating basis. The parents were very concerned about the needs of their individual youngsters and tended to focus consistently on these to the exclusion of goals for the group. Patty knew she had to find ways, other than her own say-so, to convince families about needed changes. To achieve this end, Patty called upon her graduate school instructors for input. She met individually with specialists in science, mathematics, language curriculum, and child development from the university. Each provided approaches to utilize in modeling for and interacting with parents. Several volunteered their services to lead in-house training sessions for mothers and fathers of the children in the program. The inservice workshops were an enormous success. The programmatic changes that Patty had hoped to accomplish gradually began to take shape.

This is one example of the ways that professional expertise may be utilized to achieve staff-development goals. However, there are resources to be found in the community surrounding an early childhood center as well.

SAMPLE: *Using Training Resources (Community)*
Joan B. is the principal of a small, private primary school. She recently learned that several major businesses, including a computer manufac-

turer and a school equipment firm, were offering mini grants to those schools preparing the best proposals for use of the funds. A member of the local business women's group and the Chamber of Commerce, Joan has met and formed associations with a wide range of local business persons. Among her new colleagues is the director of development for a local pharmaceutical manufacturer. Joan is aware that proposal development and grant administration are among the roles her friend plays. So Joan called upon John P. to discuss the mini-grant proposals. When John learned of the potential value to the school of the grant money, he offered to conduct a grant-writing workshop for Joan's staff. Meanwhile, Joan learned of the school adoption program designed to encourage businesses and schools to work together. She and John decided to explore how they might work together in other ways.

Joan's school benefits from her interaction with members of the community, and so will the pharmaceutical company now working along with her. Community resources may be present in the form of local merchants, as well as executives and health and human service professionals. Directors might consider developing partnerships with these members of the community: physicians, nurses, social workers, psychologists, attorneys, store clerks, pharmacists, grocers, mail delivery personnel, dentists, newspaper delivery persons, gas station operators, construction-business owners, farmers, and the like. Networking in the community opens doors and creates learning opportunities for everyone.

# CHAPTER 6

# Program Directors as Staff Trainers

OFTENTIMES, early childhood centers operate on small budgets. Directors must, therefore, have clear and financially realistic goals for all program components. Despite the fact that an outside consultant can bring new ideas and perspective to a program, hiring a training specialist is not always a director's option. Furthermore, in some areas, the program administrator is the person most attuned to the situations and human needs that promote the training activity. But there are a great many factors that influence the effectiveness of the director as trainer. Considering how to maximize the success of training efforts becomes one of the primary concerns of the early childhood administrator.

## THE DIRECTOR-STAFF RELATIONSHIP

It seems a simple statement to suggest that the most effective trainer is one who communicates well with training participants. It is also true that we all tend to listen better to persons we like, respect, and value for their expertise. In the case of the early childhood administrator who is contemplating providing staff training, this relationship is doubly important. Not only the outcomes of training, but also future staff relations may rest upon the manner in which this staff development activity is planned and undertaken.

Even prior to the onset of training, the characteristics of the previously established director-staff relationship must be taken into consideration. Some hard questions must be asked and answered, and solutions may need to be found to relational problems before staff training can be undertaken.

Figure 6–1 represents some evaluative questions to be considered by directors contemplating leadership staff development activities. These questions deal with the current state of personnel relations.

Questions like these are important for a variety of reasons. Staff are more likely to be receptive to the director as trainer if ordinary interactions are of a positive nature. Since training is a form of feedback from trainer to participants, it is helpful for the staff to be accustomed to regular feedback from their director. Previous feedback should have been of the sort designed to facilitate improvement in staff performance and provide input of a positive, "You are doing a great job," nature.

Questions aimed at a director's awareness of staffs' professional needs will help to establish whether staff will be receptive to the idea of the admin-

## DIRECTOR'S SELF-EVALUATION CHECKLIST

_____ 1. What are the characteristics of my present relationship with staff? Are interactions pleasant and easy, or tension-filled?

_____ 2. Do I talk frequently with staff on both formal and informal bases? How would I rate my communication skills?

_____ 3. Are staff accustomed to receiving feedback from me? What form does this feedback usually take (director-staff conferences, informal conversations, etc.)?

_____ 4. How aware am I of the levels of professional development of each member of my staff? Can I list at least two developmental needs of each staff member?

_____ 5. Do I have an open-door policy with regard to staff? How accessible am I on a daily basis? Do staff take advantage of this policy? How frequently?

_____ 6. Are staff accustomed to having input in some decision-making activities of the program, or do I make most decisions entirely on my own?

_____ 7. Do staff come voluntarily to discuss programmatic concerns with me?

_____ 8. Am I aware of personal or personnel problems that could interfere with the outcomes of training?

**FIGURE 6–1**

istrator's involvement in training. That is, it is easier to reach and deal with growth needs through training when the director has been actively involved in staff development on an ongoing basis.

In order for staff to accept the director as a trainer, there must also be a clear chain of command with the administrator firmly established as the leader of the program. In situations where decision making is always shared with staff, it may be difficult for staff to accept an administrator in a clear-cut leadership role, such as that of a training facilitator.

Last, but not least, there must be awareness of any staff tensions or at-home problems that would negatively color training outcomes. The authors have experienced many training situations in which concerns about program stability, salaries, ill family members, or other problems have interrupted or distracted participants from the topic at hand. A lack of awareness of difficulties like these can be a serious deterrent to training success.

## HOW TO IDENTIFY AND INFORM STAFF OF TRAINING NEEDS

The method of identifying training needs is a second factor influencing the effectiveness of the director's role as trainer. It has a two-fold impact. If staff development needs are discussed purely for the purpose of generating training topics, rather than on the basis of specific information obtained by the director, staff are likely to be less comfortable with and even resistant to training and other development activities. The authors have been acquainted with several early childhood administrators who have an annual staff training day. At other times of the year little or no attention is paid to professional growth.

If, on the other hand, training is a natural step in a regular multifaceted staff development program, then it will more likely be a welcomed part of staff-director interactions. Some suggestions follow for activities that lead naturally to needs-assessment and training and that make the director's role as trainer a more acceptable part of this process:

- *Regular staff meetings*—including time for staff to raise and discuss concerns regarding any aspect of the program.
- *Classroom observations*—conducted at frequent intervals by the program director. Staff should receive both written and verbal feedback as a result of these observations.
- *Director modeling*—of appropriate techniques for use in the classroom, in teacher-parent interactions, and for other potentially problematic situations.
- *Informal meetings*—between director and staff on a one-to-one basis for the purpose of sharing information and concerns.

- *Conference, workshop, seminar attendance*—by all staff in order for an exchange of ideas, new methods of problem solving, and new techniques to be introduced. Staff must also be encouraged to share these experiences when they return to the center.
- *Assigned and informal professional reading*—for discussion at staff meetings and for use in overall program and curriculum development.
- *Regular staff evaluations*—of a formal nature, completed by the director and providing staff with useful feedback and opportunities to discuss the director's assessment of their performance.

If these activities are ongoing, staff receive the message that their developmental needs are of importance to the program administrator. Training needs are gradually apparent to all, not merely to the director.

The next step in identifying training needs involves informing the staff of the decision to provide training. When the director is a knowledgeable professional, looked to as the program's leader, this decision can be made and the staff informed with very little occasion for debate. It is similarly helpful if the decision to offer training is part of a series of staff development events designed to achieve the same ends, such as observations at other centers for the purpose of learning new approaches to old problems. Room for staff input can be left in areas such as selection of training days and times, specific areas of staff interest, and issues for problem solving.

## STAFF AWARENESS OF PROFESSIONAL NEEDS AND GOALS

Just as the director develops a keen awareness of staff strengths and weaknesses through the previously described activities, so do individual staff members grow to understand their professional needs. With the assistance of the director, staff can become comfortable with their skills levels and learn to develop goals appropriate to present and future job responsibilities.

## LEVELS OF STAFF STRESS AND BURNOUT

As was previously discussed, the impact of personal or family problems can be quite negative. Even more problematic is that these can lead to the very high stress levels and rates of burnout common to human services personnel. Stress syndromes are often evidenced by fatigue and low energy levels, lack of creativity and initiative, and even health problems. When these symptoms become chronic, then burnout may be imminent.

It is important for an early childhood administrator to accept that training is not a cure-all for stress and burnout problems. Although staff development can be a useful tool for responding to these syndromes, it is often helpful to delay training until the roots of stress problems can be exposed and dealt with at a variety of levels: administrative, programmatic, and personal.

Staff stress and burnout are important to all because they eventually involve everyone in the program: administrators, teachers, support staff, children, and parents. Figure 6–2 shows an example of one way to measure levels of stress among early childhood staff. It may be helpful to distribute these, ask staff to rate themselves, and then discuss the implications of each of the checklist items.

## SUCCESS OF OTHER PROGRAM COMPONENTS

When an early childhood administrator considers assuming the role of training facilitator, it may be helpful to review the success rate of other program components. If results of other efforts have been less than satisfactory, one cause may be unrealistic goals or expectations. Setting goals that are too high, or that should be considered long-term, can produce disillusionment.

If negative messages have been conveyed because other problem-solving efforts have been a disappointment, staff may be skeptical about the outcomes of training even before it gets underway. Identifying short-term training objectives and assuring staff that the responsibility for achieving these is one shared by everyone can help to promote interest and involvement in the training process.

## DIRECTOR SUITABILITY AS A TRAINER

We come finally to the question that is sometimes the most difficult to answer honestly: "For the type of staff training I have in mind, am I the most suitable trainer?"

This question can only be answered by considering several important others.

- Have I had training in the area in which I would like to provide staff training?
- Have I had experiences that would help me to understand the various points of view of staff on training issues?
- How well do I communicate my ideas to others? Do I speak clearly? Am I a good listener?
- Can I accept disagreement from those I supervise?
- Have I taught or trained adult learners before?
- Do I know specific techniques for planning staff-appropriate training?

# CHECK YOUR TEACHING STRESS LEVEL

*Directions:* We all experience some level of stress in our work and personal lives. Occasionally, however, stress overwhelms us and we exhibit physical, psychological, and behavioral symptoms that are indicators that something is wrong. These symptoms may not be easy for us to see in ourselves, although family, co-workers, and friends may observe changes in us.

Check each answer True or False.

|  | True | False |
|---|---|---|
| **I. Physical Symptoms** | | |
| A. I am always tired. | _____ | _____ |
| B. I am often sick or in pain. | _____ | _____ |
| C. I have regular headaches. | _____ | _____ |
| D. I have recently gained (or lost) a lot of weight. | _____ | _____ |
| E. I have trouble sleeping at night. | _____ | _____ |
| F. When I eat my stomach becomes upset. | _____ | _____ |
| G. I spend a lot of time sleeping. | _____ | _____ |
| **II. Psychological Symptoms** | | |
| A. I dislike getting up in the morning. | _____ | _____ |
| B. I often feel depressed or sad and do not know why. | _____ | _____ |
| C. I feel unattractive. | _____ | _____ |
| D. I am dissatisfied with my life. | _____ | _____ |
| E. I often feel I would like to escape from my responsibilities. | _____ | _____ |
| F. Few people care about me. | _____ | _____ |
| G. People cannot get along without me. | _____ | _____ |
| **III. Behavioral Symptoms** | | |
| A. I do not get along with my co-workers. | _____ | _____ |
| B. I often argue with members of my family. | _____ | _____ |
| C. I have to do most things myself or they will not get done. | _____ | _____ |
| D. I have a drink every day to relax. | _____ | _____ |
| E. Drugs make me feel more confident/comfortable with myself. | _____ | _____ |
| F. Other people make my life difficult. | _____ | _____ |
| G. I have trouble making my needs known to others. | _____ | _____ |

If you check more than two items in any category, your stress level may be too high.

**FIGURE 6–2**

- Can I accept negative feedback from staff relative to my administrative role?
- Am I patient enough to wait for training results?

Answers to these self-evaluative questions may help a director to ascertain whether he or she can be an effective trainer. If some of the questions prove to be too difficult to answer, some administrators may find it helpful to talk these items over with a colleague who is familiar with their work and background. Self-evaluation is difficult at best, but it can be made easier with the assistance of an associate whose skills and opinion are valued.

## BALANCING MULTIPLE ROLES: THE STRESS FACTOR

Many early childhood administrators carry a heavy burden of responsibilities even without including staff training among their duties. Many directors work long hours for little pay and have few support systems, a situation which adds up to stress and may lead to job dissatisfaction. Making the decision to provide training can have an important and beneficial impact on staff, but a director must take positive steps to assure that assuming this new role does not mean that the program's leader is further overburdened.

What things can an administrator do to prevent stress and burnout when playing such a wide variety of roles? The following are suggested:

1. Learn to delegate authority. Do not be afraid to turn over some tasks to others who are competent and responsible.
2. Become a diligent planner and organizer. Knowing all of the steps you must follow to accomplish goals, such as those involved in providing a staff training program, can relieve tension and make work progress smoothly.
3. Develop and utilize a support system. Meet with trusted colleagues on a regular basis to share problems and ideas. Remember that professional loneliness is a frequent cause of stress.
4. Attend conferences, outside workshops, or enroll in a college course. Keep your creative juices flowing and your ideas fresh.
5. Avoid mixing professional and personal lives. Make certain to have personal time on a daily basis and be wary of becoming a workaholic.
6. Learn to prioritize. Recognize which tasks are urgent, those which can be delayed, and those which are related to short-term versus long-term goals.
7. Treat all program components equally. Avoid becoming overinvolved in a training project, for example, at the expense of other responsibilities.

8. Accept that human beings—children, parents, and staff—are and should always be an administrator's top priority. Never allow tasks to interfere with the delicate balance of relationships with others. A loyal, supportive, knowledgeable staff, working together with their director, can solve almost any problem.

## THE BENEFITS OF HAVING DIRECTORS AS TRAINERS

Although not always immediately apparent, there are distinct advantages to a director's assumption of a staff training role. The program's administrator is more likely to be familiar with staff, their skills, professional background and experiences, personalities, and special needs. These insights are not ones that an outside training consultant is privy to, nor can they be learned in a short period of time.

The early childhood director is also able to observe and learn the inner workings of the staff as a unit. That is, how do teaching partners in the same classrooms work together, and do these teams interact favorably with others in the center? What sort of planning and collaborative activities do staff get involved in? An intuitive director will also examine his or her personal impact on these interactions.

A third benefit associated with the director-trainer role is one derived from previously established relationships. Outside trainers must often spend considerable time establishing their interest in and bonds of trust with trainees. Even when much time is devoted to this effort, the consultant may remain uncertain of staff reactions to the training activity and the trainer. These responses will be more apparent and readable to someone familiar with all of those persons, as the program's director often is.

When training is conducted by a program's leader, it is often possible for questions, issues, and concerns to be raised that might not be discussed with an outside consultant. Of course, this open type of interaction would also depend greatly upon the tone set by the training facilitator. If staff fear repercussions from the discussion of problems, then issues of considerable impact may never be raised.

Not the least of possible advantages of the director-trainer role is related to training evaluation. The trainer who is also a staff supervisor is in the unique position of being able to study both the immediate and long-range impacts of staff development activities. Continuation of regular program evaluation, classroom observations, and many varieties of staff communication can help the early childhood administrator measure those aspects of staff training that have been most useful, that require revision or repetition, that most address the program's goals, and that have motivated staff and sparked creativity and teamwork.

## RECOMMENDED READING

Farber, B. A. "Psychologist Says Schools Can Reduce Their Teacher Burnout," *TC (Teachers College) Today*, Vol. 10, No. 2, Spring 1982.

Hennig, M., and A. Jardim. *The Managerial Woman*. New York: Doubleday and Company, Inc., 1976.

Hildebrand, V. *Management of Child Development Centers*. New York: Collier Macmillan Publishers, 1984.

Jorde, P. *Avoiding Burnout: Strategies for Managing Time, Space, and People in Early Childhood Education*. Washington, D.C.: Acropolis Books, 1983.

Katz, L. G. *Talks with Teachers*. Washington, D. C.: National Association for the Education of Young Children, 1977.

Mager, R. F. *Preparing Instructional Objectives*, Second Edition. Belmont, CA: Fearon-Pitman Publishers, Inc., 1975.

Maslach, C., and A. Pines, "The Burn-Out Syndrome in the Day Care Setting," *Child Care Quarterly*, Vol. 6, No. 2, Summer 1977.

McGreal, T. L. *Successful Teacher Evaluation*. Alexandria, VA: Association for Supervision and Curriculum Development, 1983.

"Why Directors Burn Out?," *Child Care Information Exchange*, September 1979, pp. 6–8.

# CHAPTER 7

# Using Outside Consultants to Meet Staff Development Needs

IN CHAPTER 6 we discussed the early childhood director's potential and role as staff trainer. A great many programs do not have the option of contracting with consultant services to meet staff development needs. Unfortunately, programs for young children are low on the priority lists of federal, state, and local governments, businesses, and many communities. Salaries are low, and continuing education for teachers and caregivers is an item absent from many an early childhood program budget. Many directors have turned to fundraising events to support their staff development component. Cake sales support everything from the purchase of journals to conference attendance to the purchase of consultant services for training.

In this chapter, we will focus on the decision to utilize consultant services for staff development, the consultant-selection process, and follow-up of consultant-led staff training activities.

## WHY HIRE A CONSULTANT?

Most early childhood directors would probably agree that at some point in time, a program needs stimulus: a breath of fresh air to promote its growth. But administrators do not stimulate programs; instead we motivate people to develop and change. The key question for many administrators is how best to promote and facilitate that development. We have noted that directors must ask themselves hard questions as they determine their suitability as trainers of their own personnel. There are issues of ability to communicate effectively, levels of current responsibility, stress factors, a director's areas of expertise, and availability of funds to pay consultants to be considered. If, after all questions have been addressed, consultant services are still a possibility, there are a great many advantages to be incurred.

Consultants, when carefully selected, can bring a level of expertise not previously experienced to staff development needs. Program personnel may consider the acquisition of new knowledge and skills and are challenged to design mechanisms for making creative and effective adaptations.

Benefits may also be derived from staff's opportunity to see themselves from the viewpoint of an outsider. This is both a frightening and exhilarating process. Directors can help to prepare staff for this experience by facilitating the outlook that a chance has arisen to identify strengths and weaknesses. If staff become defensive about what is learned, less learning and positive output is likely.

An experienced consultant may view problems and needs from a more objective viewpoint than staff or the program administrator. At times, the investments of time and energy that go into the running of day-to-day operations of an early childhood program can prevent seeing situations and individuals in the clearest way. A fresh perspective, if one is open to it, can do wonders toward rejuvenating flagging enthusiasm. Directors, too, must refrain from becoming defensive when suggestions for improvement are made.

Figure 7–1 summarizes the circumstances under which a consultant may be necessary.

## IDENTIFYING STAFF DEVELOPMENT CONSULTANTS

Consultants should be as carefully chosen as members of an early childhood program staff. With the realization that a development consultant can have a significant impact on the thinking, behavior, and interactions of all members of the staff, the key to choosing the right consultant is the establishment of hiring criteria.

### The Selection Process

Criteria should be based upon the staff development goals, the immediate objectives of development activities, and the needs of staff members. Of course, cost is not an insignificant factor. The consultant must be able to provide services at a fee reasonable to the center. Criteria should be very specific in nature and written for discussion with potential consultants, staff, parents, and board members.

In the following sections of this chapter, two examples are provided of staff development needs. Each of these is followed by a description of the consultant qualifications (hiring criteria) that might be identified in order to meet stated needs.

> *Situation #1:* Barbara P. is the headmistress at Willow Valley Primary Academy. She has held this position for five years, although there has recently been a significant turnover of other staff. Barbara has noted that there is a lack of cohesiveness with regard to curriculum planning and implementation. Teachers seem to be utilizing curriculum models and methods according to their own interests and needs, rather than following the open education philosophy traditionally espoused by the school. There has been a drop in grades in all classrooms, and parents have complained to Barbara that they no longer understand the goals of the program. Barbara has tried in several ways to address the problem, speaking to the need for curriculum consistency in staff meetings and observing in all classrooms to provide feedback on teacher styles and skills. The problem has persisted. Barbara no longer feels competent to respond to the situation and is seeking an outside consultant. She thinks

## CONSULTANTS AS STAFF DEVELOPERS

Consultants may make the best staff developers when:

—present staff lack the appropriate expertise to meet development needs

—the director and other administrative staff are already overloaded with responsibility and cannot undertake additional tasks

—staff stress levels are high, morale is low, and revitalization is sought

—personnel communication and interaction problems exist

—a major program change is mandated

—there is a clear need for leadership in some program component area that no staff member has been able to assume

—a personnel or programmatic problem has been ongoing and unresolvable to date

—an unfamiliar approach or techniques must be presented

—new directions or fresh perspectives are sought

—director is not the appropriate person to respond to a staff development need

**FIGURE 7–1**

that the observation and training provided by a skilled individual might resolve the curriculum problems.

## Recommended Consultant Qualifications

a. Education: An advanced degree in early childhood education, curriculum theory, or curriculum and instruction.

b. Teacher/Administrative Experience: Minimum of five years classroom teaching experience; minimum of two years teaching in open classroom setting; minimum two years in administrative capacity in an open education program.

c. Philosophy: Compatible with that of the Willow Valley Primary Academy.

d. Publications/Research: Study of open education implementation problems would be an asset to staff-developer skills.

e. Consulting Experience: Minimum of one year higher-education teaching or adult-education experience.

f. Personal Characteristics: Professional manner and appearance; positive and assertive in interactions with others; excellent communication skills.

## Rationale for Criteria Identified

a. Many individuals both in and outside the field mistakenly believe that degrees in early childhood, elementary education, and child development are interchangeable. In this particular situation the need to distinguish between these types of professional training is critical. A child developmentalist has expertise in the theories, research, and observation of the physical, cognitive, social, and emotional growth of children. Early childhood and elementary educators, on the other hand, have knowledge of curriculum models and innovations. Therefore, the latter group of specialists are preferred as consultants to address the problem at the Academy.

b. The second of the consultant qualifications deals with an individual's teaching and administrative background. If a consultant has not had at some point the same responsibilities as those persons that he or she is advising, a credibility gap may develop. The consultant may not understand the real nature of the problems experienced and will communicate this to staff in some way. Having been in the shoes of both teacher and administrator is a valuable asset to understanding the perspective of program staff.

c. The reasons for philosophical agreement are fairly obvious. While it is highly desirous for new ideas to be introduced, thoughts that are in direct opposition to the basic tenets of the program can create dissension.

d. Research and publications are the two criteria for consultant hiring that may be considered flexible in this instance. A great deal of insight could be derived from teaching and administration, but additional study of open education through the research or writing modalities would be an added bonus.

e. Previous consulting experience is a must, although we do have a somewhat broad definition of this. If an individual has been an adult educator at some level, he or she has learned the process and skills for identifying grown-up (as opposed to children's) learning styles. There is, for example, a great difference between teaching in the preschool classroom and working with middle school children. The differences are magnified ten-fold when one works with adults, and a consultant must be attuned to these variances.

f. The final group of qualifications are personal characteristics. The first attribute noticed by most people in Western Culture is appearance. It is the human cover by which most of us are first judged. An air of professionalism (not elitism) is a tool that can carry the message of authority and expertise with it. On the other hand, confusing academic jargon or a condescending manner can be a deterrent to the success of staff-development activity.

> *Situation #2:* Lincoln Preschool is a Title XX-funded day-care program in a large eastern city. Matt W. has been the executive director of the program for only six months. He feels very positively about his new position, as well as the teachers and support staff he supervises. Matt feels strongly that the parent involvement component of the program could be improved. Parents rarely attend meetings scheduled for them, and participation by families in home-school events is almost nonexistent. Matt is certain that part of the problem stems from the attitude of the teachers toward parents. All of the parents are employed, and many are single mothers. Work and child-rearing schedules leave little time for visits to school. If staff could look at parent involvement in a different light, Matt feels, some change might be achieved in this component. As a man, Matt is not sure he is the best person to address the maternal-child issues involved. He plans to hire a consultant to conduct staff training on parent involvement.

## Recommended Consultant Qualifications

a. Education: An advanced degree in early childhood education, social work, or family dynamics

b. Teaching/Administrative Experience: Minimum of two years working in a teaching or administrative capacity with families in the day-care setting; minimum of three years working with families in a social service/therapeutic/health care setting

c. Philosophy: Compatible with that of the Lincoln Preschool

d. Publications/Research: Study or publication of information on parent-child relationships, changes in family life, or home-school relationships would be valuable.

e. Consulting Experience: Minimum of one year higher education teaching or other adult-education experience

f. Personal Characteristics: Professional manner and experience; positive and assertive in interactions with others; excellent communication skills

## Rationale for Criteria Identified

a. The emphasis in this consultant search is to locate an individual with an understanding of the needs of working parents. Early childhood educators, social workers, and therapists are among those who have the background and experience in work with families to respond to this staff development need.

On the other hand, the consultant selected must have a basic understanding of the parent-caregiver relationships that develop in the day-care setting. For this reason some experience in day care is essential. Additional years in a health or human services program, which provides different insight into family needs, would be highly desirable.

b–f. Philosophic, consulting experience, and personal characteristics requirements remain the same. Where research and publication background is concerned, this is once again an optional criteria. Since some of the family life changes are relatively new trends, a consultant must be up to date on the most recent findings.

## The Consultant-Learning Process

If consultants are to be utilized for in-house training or other staff development activities, a director must devote some time to singling out that person or persons who are best suited to the task at hand. This can be a time-taking procedure, but it need not be complicated. The screening process suggested for selecting a consultant is as follows:

1. Following the steps outlined in Chapters 1 and 4, the director should know what the staff development needs are. Admittedly, there are times when assistance is required with this. But no outside person is ever aware in the way an administrator can be of the group dynamics, personalities, and other factors at work in early childhood programs. As much as is possible, a narrowing-down process should be undertaken before consultant assistance is requested.

2. Recommendations for consultants should be sought. Good sources of referrals are local colleges and universities, businesses, health care, and education programs. If colleagues have utilized consultant services, their suggestions may be the most reliable.

3. Solicit vita and proposals for staff development from a small, select group of consultants. Review these carefully, considering the qualifications of applicants, feasibility of plans, their correlation to staff development goals, and fee charged (see Figure 7–2).

4. Interview the two or three persons who seem to have the skills and ideas that are needed. Assess their essential personal characteristics at this time, and solicit their answers to several key questions related to their potential roles as program consultants.

5. If possible, discuss the choices with the staff, and request their suggestions. Remember, however, that the final decision rests with the program's administrator.

6. Make the decision about which consultant best meets human and program needs and notify that individual. Be certain to notify in writing those not selected and thank them for their time and the information provided about their services.

Please note that there are circumstances under which all of the steps in the consultant screening process may not be necessary. For example: directors may have many opportunities to interact with experts in the field, attend conference workshop sessions, or hear lectures given specifically for administrators. These are often the settings where potential consultants can be located. The director can gauge personal characteristics, speaking ability, expertise, and audience impact of the presenter. Additional information is usually available during the interview.

## Briefing the Consultant

The final step in the process of retaining a consultant is providing an in-depth briefing of the objectives to be realized and any barriers to them. The chances for staff developers to be effective are reduced when information about the unique circumstances and persons to be involved is withheld.

Briefing a consultant should be a collaborative event. During this time director and consultant share information, describe personal needs and identify roles to be played that will facilitate the success of their efforts. Examples of the sort of collaboration possible include:

| *Director* | *Consultant* |
|---|---|
| "Please address these ___, ___, ___ issues in your presentation." | "I will need these materials for the first sessions in order to do that. Can you provide them?" |
| "I would like to attend your sessions with staff on ___ and ___." | "I would appreciate your involvement. What role would you like to play at those times?" |

"Can we meet on ____ to discuss your classroom observations?"

"I will be available at (time). It is good to keep one another informed for the duration of my work here."

"What room (space) do you think would be most conducive to the activities in the second session?"

"Why don't we walk around the center, look at the available space, and discuss it?"

## Consultant Fees

Although the selection of a training consultant should be based primarily upon an individual trainer's expertise and other skills criteria, fees charged can be a serious consideration for the program director. Since many day-care-center budgets do not include large sums for staff development, available funds must be carefully utilized.

How does an administrator determine what amount is reasonable payment for consultant services? Since consultation fees can vary greatly from one part of the country to another, and from one field to another, it may be useful for a director to take steps to assure that the fee requested is in keeping with the service provided. The first of these steps is to survey fellow administrators regarding the fees they have paid for outside training services. This can also be an excellent way of identifying the consultant with appropriate expertise.

Second, we suggest obtaining a written contract with services to be provided clearly stated, along with the cost of services. This provides legal protection for both parties. Additionally, it is recommended that the degree of experience of the trainer should be a factor in the fee paid. An individual with considerable consultation background would be justified in charging a higher fee than someone with less experience.

Last, we would recommend that unless a director has been referred to a trainer by a colleague, he or she should request references from previous consulting clients.

## COLLEGE COURSES AS A STAFF DEVELOPMENT OPTION

We have suggested several times that in-house consultation is not always the appropriate avenue for staff development. Many institutions of higher learning offer the alternatives of certificate, credentialing, and two-year and four-year degree programs that address both programmatic and individual goals for professional growth. When the center budget will be used to pay staff tuitions at local colleges, the director has some responsibility to explore available programs and departments and advise students about what may be available.

## SAMPLE MATERIAL AVAILABLE FROM CONSULTANT

**Creative Programs Associates***
**263 W. Broad Street**
**Pleasant Town, NJ 12334**
**Tel. (555) 555-1234**

CREATIVE PROGRAMS ASSOCIATES, an educational consulting and training partnership, now makes available to early childhood education programs and child-care agencies workshops designed to meet the training needs of your program. Program directors may select from the topics that follow, or may request a more individualized training approach. Please telephone (555) 555-1234 if you wish to schedule training, or if we can answer any questions you have about our program.

### The Trainers
John Smith, Ed.D., and Margaret Wilson Smith, Ed.D., are early childhood educators with a combination of 35 years of teaching and training experience. They have held positions as classroom teachers, program directors, and currently as college instructors at Community College and Chestnut Street College. Their consulting firm, CREATIVE PROGRAMS ASSOCIATES, has provided training and given lectures for agencies and organizations such as Association for Childhood Education International, Educators' Roundtable, and the Early Childhood Resource Center of the New York Public Library. They are the authors of articles in several national publications including the *Target Educational System* and *Child Care Journal*.

### The Workshops
Each of the following workshops as described is 1 hour, 45 minutes in length, unless otherwise indicated. Each provides for group interaction, as well as a question-and-answer period at the workshop's conclusion. Workshops are designed to deal with practical problems faced by early childhood personnel and attempt to foster each individual's arrival at solutions and techniques that fit his or her own needs. Workshops may be scheduled at a variety of times to permit maximum staff attendance. The cost of each workshop session is ____ and includes a bibliography of resources for each participant. If a workshop you desire is not listed, please inquire and describe your needs for training.

*Developing Teaching Partnerships*—stresses the value of "partnering" between teachers and parents in the early childhood setting. Describes the components of the partnership relationship and practical techniques for making it work. Discusses common problems, such as work-related stress, and parent and teacher burnout.

*Developing Cognitive Skills During the Preschool Years*—describes an approach for developing a variety of concepts and skills (such as classification, comparison and contrast, experimentation, recognition of patterns, etc.) through five main curriculum areas: language, mathematics, science, social studies, and health. Ideas are suggested to promote use of an "integrated" curriculum.

*Names, organization, address, and telephone are fictitious.

**FIGURE 7–2**

*Promoting Positive Behavior in Preschool Children*—focuses on the responsibilities and roles of teachers as they help children develop cooperative, responsible behaviors. Techniques for responding to specific behavior problems and producing appropriate, consistent responses from adult caregivers will also be discussed.

*Using Outdoor Learning Spaces*—using the outdoors for learning in all skills areas is the subject of this workshop. Reasons preschool teachers fail to use the outdoor environment and suggestions for specific activities in all types of weather are provided.

*Leadership Roles for Early Childhood Educators*—designed specifically for the head teacher or program director, this workshop is aimed at providing open discussion of management of early childhood programs and includes issues such as identifying needs of families, working with parents, dealing successfully with personnel problems, using community resources effectively, and evaluating and modifying programs (two sessions).

Other Workshops Available:
    Promoting Parent Involvement in Early Childhood Education
    Developing Observing and Record-Keeping Skills
    Promoting Language Arts Development in the 3–5 Year Old
    Identifying Learning and Health Problems in Young Children
    The Child Development Associate Credential: The Application, Portfolio
    Preparation, and Assessment Processes

**FIGURE 7–2 cont'd.**

## Investigating Local College Programs

While in some areas of the country selection of staff development-appropriate courses may be limited to one of two colleges with suitable offerings, urban areas may have numerous possibilities, such as early childhood education training programs, child development and child-care departments, family day-care certificates, and training that prepares learners for Child Development Associate assessment. Such a wide array of choices can be confusing to those who have never attended college before. So, while learning about academic resources, an early childhood administrator can obtain essential information about each college program.

An early childhood education department is probably the kind likely to offer the most appropriate courses, but suitable alternatives may also be found in child development, child-care, human development, psychology, and human services programs. A current college catalog usually contains both program or departmental requirements and course descriptions. Visits to local campuses and facilities to study facilities and college atmosphere can also be useful.

## Meeting with College Representatives

When the college course option for staff development has been selected, college faculty may be viewed as potential consultants. A director should meet with faculty to explore the direction and purposes of the various departments. Of special interest to those who supervise teachers and caregivers would be the types of support and advising systems available to students. When adults with work and family responsibilities return to school, possibility exists for several outcomes. If the support systems are in place and active in all three critical environments (work, home, and school), stress is kept to a minimum. Adult learners have a good chance to succeed and benefit from their college educations. If, on the other hand, essential support systems are absent, stress may mount and a sense of frustration, ending in failure to complete school work, may result.

There are several varieties of counseling and advising services available in college settings. Some are general in nature, conducted in a campuswide advising center. That which is most helpful to continuing-education students is inner departmental. This type makes advisors of the same faculty that provide course instruction. Professors get to know students' problems, learning styles and special needs intimately. The students feel supported personally and academically, rather than being lost in a large computerized system.

The advising issue is one example of the types of questions to be addressed to the representatives of colleges when meeting with them. Here are some of the additional queries to be answered about college courses on behalf of staff and director:

- At what hours are courses offered? On which days?
- How recently did faculty have their last experiences as teachers or administrators of early childhood program?
- Are observations of other preschool and primary programs recommended?
- Are credits awarded for students' life experience, especially present work experience? If so, what are the criteria for assessment of experience?
- What facilities do part-time students have access to?
- Is financial aid available when the center cannot pay the full price of tuition?
- What sort of assignments are routinely given? Are remedial classes available if assistance is needed with basic skills?
- Is reading required? If so, what is the cost of materials or texts to be purchased by students?
- Does any sort of confidentiality rule apply between students and faculty that is designed to inhibit discussion of problems at students' centers?
- What are the percentages of preservice and inservice students in the department?

## Selecting Appropriate Courses for Staff Development

As much as possible, staff should be urged to select their own courses, on the basis of perceived need, interest, or their advising plans. This is part of the important business of encouraging the growth of independence and individually developed professional growth plans. It is also somewhat egotistical to assume that no staff are capable of making their own course selections and that all must have it done for them.

Occasionally, however, there are unique group needs that an administrator can arrange for. For instance:

> An academic institution with which one of the authors is familiar has a number of health and human service affiliate programs. In one of these the staff were polled to determine their perceptions of staff training needs. It was decided that all levels of staff in this program for

exceptional persons would benefit from a child-development course. The proper department was contacted, and because of the distance between the college and the program in question, as well as the number of persons to be trained, the college decided to send a faculty member to the work site to conduct the course. Tuition was paid by the students' agency. In all other respects it was the same course as that taught on campus, but it did address the needs of a specific group of child-care workers. The single course was a great success from the students' standpoint, and several decided to work toward the degree offered by the college at their own expense.

In this, as in other similar cases, the course-selection process is almost identical to those recommended for identifying staff development needs and consultants. The steps are:

1. Gather data about staff development needs (observe, discuss, assess)
2. Develop goals and objectives to meet those needs
3. Formulate a plan to address aims (which course is most likely to result in goal achievement?)
4. Identify persons (faculty) and other resources to implement plan
5. Develop a timetable for implementation
6. Implement the program
7. Evaluate outcomes (learning) along the way and modify the plan as needed (more on this in Chapter 11)

## EXPECTATIONS FOR CONSULTANT SERVICES

An administrator who is unfamiliar with the processes of identifying and arranging for outside trainers may also be unaware of what the consultant contract entitles him or her to. Obviously, the more that is spelled out in the contract, the better the protection for both the center and the consultant. The areas that should be addressed in precontractural discussion as well as in the contract document are:

1. The content of training, or the specific nature of the service to be provided (e.g., observations of the classroom and written recommendations to improve program quality)
2. The techniques to be used by the consultant (i.e., lecture or workshop format with group discussion)
3. The materials to be provided or utilized by the consultant in the provision of services, including workshop materials or handouts

4. The process of accountability, which is especially important, as it establishes the degree to which the consultant is responsible for the outcomes of training

Directors should bear in mind that a trainer cannot guarantee changes in behavior of staff, nor can improvements in program quality be assured. However, a director can hold a trainer responsible for skills development. Whatever evaluative measures are utilized to ascertain the results of training, the role and responsibility of consultant for these should be carefully spelled out.

## Following up Consultant-led Activities

Directors should never divorce themselves from the work of a retained staff development consultant. Not only should administrators be present for training when it is offered, but they should meet regularly with the trainer to discuss short-term objectives, outcomes, and future plans. It would be convenient to say that once consultant services are rendered, all goals are achieved and skills mastered, but that is seldom the case. Few of us, young or old, bright or not so bright, learn without practice and positive reinforcement. In a nutshell, these are the follow-up tasks of the director.

Administrators must provide the opportunities for staff to exercise newly learned talents in constructive and satisfying ways. Verbal and other reinforcement must be meted out in approrpriate amounts so that once stimulating ideas do not suffer atrophy and wither away.

Children, parents, policy board members, and the community should be invited to witness the positive impact of staff development activities through a "see how we have grown" approach.

Americans of the 1980s are consumer-oriented, anxious to learn what their hard-earned money can purchase. We want services that produce a visible product, and so it should be. But not unlike healthy seedlings, without nurturance and a chance to bask in the sun, early childhood staff will not flourish in their environment.

### RECOMMENDED READING

Kennedy, A., "One Perspective on the Consulting Process," *Exchange*, Vol. 4, No. 3, Summer 1979.

Kiester, A. J. *Consultation in Day Care.* Chapel Hill, NC: Institute of Government of North Carolina, 1969.

Kilman, R. H., and I. I. Mitroff, "Problem Defining and the Consulting/ Intervention Process," *California Management Review,* Vol. 21, No. 3, 1979, pp. 26–33.

Scarlett, W. G., et al, "On Using Consultants: Suggestions for Administrators and Teachers," *Child Care Information Exchange,* Vol. 11, 1980, pp. 26–29.

Stalmack, J. E., "S.W.A.P. Strategies Which Affect Programs: A Framework for Staff Development," *Young Children,* Vol. 36, No. 6, September 1981, pp. 16–24.

Swartz, S. L. and J. K. Mott. *Some Guidelines for On-Site Staff Development Activities.* Queens College Title XX Day Care Project, September 1981.

# CHAPTER 8

# A Program Model and Techniques for Performance-Based Assessment

*"In our private moments, those of us who educate adults in the human service professions have confronted our doubts about the success of our teaching. We ask ourselves if we are truly able to educate effective, empathic, and powerful professionals...When we observe our students on the job, we are reminded of the discrepancy between the mastery of theory and its successful implementation in practice."*[1]

Joan Goldsmith
Defining and Measuring Competence

AS EARLY AS the 1960s, there was a growing concern among educators regarding the skills development of their students. In the early part of this decade, the nation had been stunned into a curriculum revolution by the 1957 launching of the Russian Sputnik satellite. By the mid 1960s, the legislation was passed and funds made available, through the Elementary and Secondary Education Act of 1965, which mandated far-reaching reforms, equality of educational opportunity, and which demanded accountability of results. Accountability was the mother of the competency-based teacher education movement.

Three factors influential in the evolution of the emphasis on competency of teachers and learners were:

1. The national concern for the growing failure of schools to produce literate citizens
2. The demands of teachers for salaries, rights, and benefits benefiting their efforts
3. The consumer demand for teacher responsibility, in return for an elevation in status and professional advantage

In the past, teacher education programs were almost entirely experience based. It was assumed that a particular sequence of courses would produce the knowledge and experiences that resulted in effective teachers.

By the 1960s, however, it was clear that many teachers lacked essential skills for their work with children. Furthermore, the explosion of knowledge in many fields made it exceedingly difficult for in-service educators to keep abreast of rapid changes that could impact on curriculum content and methods of instruction.

In the 1970s, the American Association of Colleges for Teacher Education, the National Council for the Accreditation of Teacher Education, and the United States Office of Education, as well as some of the state departments of education strongly supported efforts to move from traditional modes of teacher education to the performance-based model.[2]

This change in approach occurred not only in elementary and secondary but in early childhood education as well. In this chapter, we will explore some of the programs that have been developed to facilitate and assess teacher skills and explore their impact upon staff development in center settings.

## A CREDENTIAL FOR PRESCHOOL PERSONNEL

By 1970, there were fast-growing numbers of nursery schools and day-care centers. The Head Start Program had celebrated its sixth birthday, and sociologists were predicting that increasing numbers of women would enter the work force, creating an expanding need for child-care facilities. Although state certification standards had long been set for elementary and secondary teachers, few states required certification at the nursery school level. At the same time, many states had set health and safety standards for day-care centers, but neglected to stipulate qualifications for staff.

In response to the concern for quality programs generated by this situation, the Administration for Children, Youth, and Families convened a meeting of spokespersons in the field of early childhood education whose role was to collaborate on the development of a new professional credential. This group came to be called the Child Development Associate Consortium (C.D.A.). The Consortium's members had two primary charges. First, they were to identify the skills and knowledge needed by the new child-care professionals. The task force was to determine the guidelines to be used in training these individuals.[3]

Within the next four years, several major steps had been taken by the Consortium members. They had identified and adopted six broad competency areas and delineated thirteen functional areas (see Figure 8–1). There were thirteen pilot training programs funded to develop and test innovative approaches to training. By 1974, the Consortium was field testing the viability of the assessment system designed to measure professional competence. By July 1977, 2,000 Child Development Associate Credentials had been awarded and 4,000 more child-care workers were enrolled in competency-based training at colleges and universities across the country. By late 1981, the number of credentialed early childhood personnel had risen to 8,000 with many states recognizing the validity of the award in their staff qualification standards.[4]

## The C.D.A. Training Program

Among those designated to design and implement one of the pilot training programs were early childhood educators based at Community College of Philadelphia, Research for Better Schools (a non-profit educational laboratory), and the School District of Philadelphia, all in Pennsylvania. In a strongly collaborative effort, these institutions had applied for and received funding from the Office of Child Development and undertook the tedious process of developing appropriate training curriculum and materials.

The program developed in Philadelphia had these major characteristics: (1) it had specified competencies that students were expected to demonstrate when their training was completed; (2) the instruction provided was primarily field, rather than college-classroom based; (3) instruction was highly individualized; and (4) the training program was broken down into a series of sequential but self-contained modules.[5]

Individuals employed in federally funded preschool programs were eligible to participate in training, and between 1973 and 1979, 75 child-care workers enrolled in the program. The training consisted of college classes, field activities, and on-site instructor supervision and consultation on a weekly

## CHILD DEVELOPMENT ASSOCIATE COMPETENCIES AND FUNCTIONAL AREAS

*Competencies\**

*Functional Areas\**

I. To establish and maintain a safe, healthy, learning environment

1. Safe
2. Healthy
3. Learning Environment

II. To advance physical and intellectual competence

4. Physical
5. Cognitive
6. Communication
7. Creative

III. To support social and emotional development and provide positive guidance and discipline

8. Self
9. Social
10. Guidance and Discipline

IV. To establish positive and productive relationships with families

11. Families

V. To ensure a well-run, purposeful program responsive to participant needs

12. Program Management

VI. To maintain a commitment to professionalism

13. Professionalism

\*Revised Version, November 1983

FIGURE 8–1

basis. Students worked at their own pace through a series of learning modules. Each module dealt with a topic correlated with one or more of the C.D.A. functional areas. In the college classroom, instructors acted as facilitators and resource persons, occasionally lecturing or showing films. Each student received both one-to-one assistance whenever needed and reinforcement for activities completed. Some of the activities were designed to be completed in small groups so that peer influence, support, and even friendly competition were factors in the learning process.

Each classroom activity was followed by a field-based mastery activity. Mastery learning was said to have occurred when the student made specific practical applications of knowledge or theory previously acquired. Mastery activities always required some specific interaction of the student (teacher) with children, co-workers, parents, or the early childhood center environment. Although not all field activities were observed by a college instructor, the results of these were reviewed by the field supervisor, and feedback and one-to-one encouragement were provided on a weekly basis. It was the completion of all of the twenty-one modules and their activities that ended the training process.

## The Credential Award System

While each of the thirteen different training programs had a unique curriculum, the Child Development Associate credentialing process was predetermined by the C.D.A. Consortium. During the training process, each candidate for the credential prepared a portfolio of materials designed to illustrate his or her competence in the thirteen functional areas. Students in the Philadelphia program were able to utilize their mastery activities as competency indicators. Designed in a fashion similar to that of Montessori teacher's albums, the portfolio contained a candidate's short biography, preschool-classroom activities, samples of children's work, photographs, and many other indices of competence in the designated areas. A candidate had to have the portfolio completed before the actual assessment meeting could occur.

Another of the candidate's tasks was to assemble a Local Assessment Team (LAT). The four individuals on the team, the candidate and three others, were those who participated in the team meeting, which was the final determinant of candidate suitability for the credential (see Figure 8–2).

There are several unique aspects of the meeting of the Local Assessment Team. For example, all members of the Team have voting privileges, even the Candidate. Even when a Candidate is judged competent by all members of the Team, recommendations for professional growth are made. In this way, the assessment meeting and the entire preparation process are part of a learning experience for the Candidate.

## ROLES OF THE LOCAL ASSESSMENT TEAM[6]

Members of the Local Assessment Team and their roles in the Credential Award System are as follows:

1. Candidate—complete the application process; select members of the Local Assessment Team; prepare a portfolio; notify the Consortium when ready for assessment; be present on the date of the assessment meeting.

2. Trainer—work along with Candidate to assure that portfolio requirements are met; complete a series of three observations of the Candidate and record these on the forms provided by the Consortium; be present for the assessment meeting and participate by giving evidence of Candidate competence in the functional areas.

3. Parent-Community Representative—observe the Candidate once and record the observation on the form provided by the Consortium; distribute to the parents of children in the Candidate's classroom a questionnaire which requests that they provide feedback regarding the Candidate's performance in the preschool classroom; collect and tally the questionnaire results; be present at the assessment meeting and participate by providing evidence of candidate competence.

4. Child Development Associate Representative—becomes an active member of the Local Assessment Team on the day of the assessment meeting; observes the Candidate the day of the final assessment; discusses the observation with the Candidate using a written record of the behaviors observed; calls the assessment meeting to order, assuring that the guidelines and requirements of the Consortium are followed; provides evidence of Candidate competence during the meeting; sends a written record of the proceedings, as well as the Team's recommendations to award or withhold the Credential to the Consortium.

FIGURE 8–2

## Implications for Staff Development

It has been suggested on several occasions that directors must be aware of the skills possessed by staff and that one of the ways in which the awareness can best be developed is through observation. We often use examples of inappropriate behavior or language as indices that staff development is needed, while failing to determine the link between missing information, understanding, and practice. If training sessions or other forms of growth-producing activity are planned, some means must be devised to help staff make the transfer of theoretical information to center classroom situations. Anyone who learns new information or a skill also needs a chance to practice, determining how best to implement ideas. There must be opportunities to make mistakes without penalty. When there has been ample practice time, appropriate feedback is essential to help staff recognize strengths and weaknesses.

Just as the Child Development Associate Credential Award System and the C.D.A. training program are skills-facilitators based upon Candidate performance, so ultimately should staff development activities be. The type of training program described serves as a reminder that individual learning styles and pace must be recognized. It is a mistake to assume that everyone in a group will grasp and make significant changes in attitude and behavior based upon a single learning opportunity. Skills learning should be treated as an ongoing experience, one that might originate with discussion, is enhanced by a training activity, and continues through practice and regular reinforcement.

Figure 8–3 provides examples of the skills caregivers in the preschool might demonstrate to indicate their competence in the areas described by the Child Development Associate Consortium. Figure 8–4 shows these developed into items on an observation form that might be utilized by a director or other staff developer to pinpoint those areas where growth is most evident or is needed.

## DEVELOPING COMPETENCY-BASED TRAINING PROGRAMS

In writing about an assessment model system of training, Joan Goldsmith (1979) suggests that there are a number of key requirements.[7]

1. The needs of both the professional, as learner, and those of the children and families served must be considered. Evaluation of client needs is essential to this training approach because it is one of the chief means by which a trainer will know the skills that caregivers must develop.

2. In competency-based programs, the assessment process cannot be separated from the training process. It must be ongoing, broadly based, and aimed at promoting maximum competence of the caregiver. Goldsmith notes that multiple-choice questions, checklists, and other forms of "passive analysis" are often used as assessment tools, rather than actual experience. Instead of

# GUIDELINES FOR PORTFOLIO PREPARATION

I. Functional Area: *Safe*

*Indoors*
A. Establishes safety rules
B. Plans for emergency exit from building (fire drills)
C. Checks equipment regularly to assure that it is in good condition
D. Checks bathroom water temperature
E. Checks floors for splinters
F. Determines that windows are screened or barred
G. Ensures that radiator or hot-water pipes are covered
H. Supervises children's play
I. Keeps medicines/cleaning fluids out of children's reach

*Outdoors*
A. Teaches safety rules applicable:
   1. on a walk
   2. on a trip
   3. in the playground
B. Keeps play area free of debris that might cause injury (glass, tree branches, etc.)

II. Functional Area: *Healthy*

*Indoors*
A. Has adequate first aid, tissue, and soap supplies available
B. Plans nutritious meals and snacks for children
C. Plans activities that encourage good health habits
   1. using toilet
   2. washing hands
   3. using tissues
   4. toothbrushing
   5. taking nap time
   6. getting adequate fresh air and sun
   7. dressing properly for outdoors
D. Assures adequate light, ventilation, heat
E. Covers trash cans
F. Provides isolation area for ill child
G. Records accidents, treatment, care given
H. Checks incoming children for signs of illness
I. Recognizes and adequately deals with children's health problems

*Outdoors*
A. Assures clean, dry play area
B. Provides play area containing no litter, open trash cans, yard tools

**FIGURE 8–3**

## III. Functional Area: *Learning Environment*

*Indoors*

A. Selects and uses materials and equipment that stimulate the children (correct developmental level)
B. Maintains a well-arranged and orderly environment (labeled, uncluttered shelves)
C. Includes materials that reflect the children's culture
D. Uses bulletin boards; displays at children's eye level
E. Uses interest centers reflecting children's interest
F. Provides equipment at correct height for children (tables, chairs, shelves, toilets)
G. Labels cubbies, cots with children's names
H. Understands uses of equipment and materials in classroom
I. Uses bright colors and makes effort to create a cheerful, stimulating environment
J. Plans room arrangements of all equipment and materials so it is well thought-out and created for learning and safety.

*Outdoors*

A. Brings indoor equipment and materials outdoors when possible
B. Arranges outdoor equipment for maximum opportunities for development by children
C. Uses outdoors as learning environment (nature walks, etc.)

## IV. Functional Area: *Physical*

*Indoors*

A. Provides equipment and materials for the development of gross motor skills
B. Provides equipment and materials for the development of fine motor skills
C. Makes adaptations to meet the needs of handicapped children
    1. observes to discover level of physical development of all children
    2. plans activities for skill development of children at all levels
    3. reports suspected physical impairments or illness to supervisory staff
D. Plans lessons and activities for the development of the five senses
E. Requests and uses equipment to aid in the physical development of the children

*Outdoors*

A. Assures outdoor play time for gross motor development (weather permitting)
B. Makes maximum use of outdoor play equipment for gross motor development

## V. Functional Area: *Cognitive*

*Indoors*

A. Helps children develop concepts related to space, time, numbers, etc. (MATH)
B. Provides materials and equipment for exploration and experimentation in SCIENCE activities
C. Provides challenging experiences that stimulate curiosity and motivate children to learn

**FIGURE 8–3 cont'd.**

D. Understands basic cognitive skills and ability to implement their development via lessons, activities, and environmental conditions
    1. classifying
    2. comparing and contrasting
    3. seeing patterns

*Outdoors*
A. Uses outdoors for implementation of SCIENCE activities
B. Uses walks, outdoor play as areas for development of MATH skills

VI. Functional Area: *Communication*

*Indoors*
A. Uses own speech as a model and provides children with opportunities for language acquisition and use
    1. uses circle and meal times for discussion
    2. uses experience stories
    3. introduces new words
    4. writes under children's drawings, art work using their words
B. Helps children associate word meaning with experiences
    1. provides a variety of types of books for children's use (story, information, reference)
    2. encourages children's imitation of adults and use of new words, providing guidance for usage
    3. provides records and tapes of songs and stories in a listening center
    4. encourages use of doll corner as a place for nonsexist dramatic play and experimentation with different kinds of language
C. Encourages verbal and nonverbal expression
    1. helps children understand uses of other media as a form of communication (drama, painting, drawing, creative movement, etc.)
D. Encourages use of child's native language in bilingual setting

*Outdoors*
A. Uses trips, walks, etc., to stimulate language through new experience, introduction of new words
NOTE: Language deals with the following skills:
    1. reading
    2. listening
    3. speaking
    4. writing

VII. Functional Area: *Creative*

*Indoors*
A. Encourages creative expression of feelings and ideas
B. Provides activities, materials, and equipment that encourage creative endeavors (art, music, dramatics, movement, etc.)
C. Helps children develop interest in expressive experience through exposure, appreciation, and communication through creative experience

**FIGURE 8–3 cont'd.**

110

D. Helps children develop creativity in all activities including:
   1. dressing-up
   2. block building
   3. sand and water play
   4. food or snack preparation
   5. redecorating doll corner, etc.
E. Helps children appreciate differences in people ("He has lovely eyes!" "She is very tall!")

*Outdoors*
A. Helps children appreciate beauty in living things and all of nature
B. Helps children notice simple differences in the architectural design of community buildings

VIII. Functional Area: *Self*

*Indoors*
A. Helps each child to have success (autonomy*) experience
B. Provides a comfortable atmosphere in which to discuss and share information on cultural heritage (identify)
C. Helps each child to become aware of and exercise control over his or her own body
D. Has understanding of key words in definition
   1. awareness (of self) is identity
   2. esteem is self-worth
E. Encourages children in development of self-help skills (getting out and replacing own materials, shoe tying, fastening and unfastening clothes)
F. Provides a balance of success experiences and challenging experiences (helps child develop autonomy and then initiative*)
G. Helps child find acceptable ways of expressing negative feelings
H. Has understanding of key words:
   1. independence (develops because child feels good about himself or herself; a sense of self-worth)
   2. responsibility (child begins to assume responsibility for his or her actions)

*Outdoors*
A. Uses neighborhood walks to help children develop a sense of awareness about their community, where each one's house is located, etc.
B. Uses playground activities to help increase children's physical skills (increases their sense of control over their bodies)
C. Encourages children to be responsible for their playthings
D. Encourages children to watch out for themselves and others on walks by recalling rules and hand holding

*Autonomy (develops ages 1 to 3 years)—child is given enough freedom by adults within limits (he or she is protected from harm) to try things on his or her own. Child gets ideas and encouragement from adults and often imitates them.
*Initiative*—child has had enough practice and successes with various tasks to try many things on his or her own with some encouragement from adults.

**FIGURE 8–3 cont'd.**

IX. Functional Area: *Social*

*Indoors*
A. Provides an environment in which children can work cooperatively with groups as well as individually
   1. knows levels of play
      a. solitary
      b. onlooker
      c. parallel
      d. associative
      e. cooperative
   2. observes to determine each child's level of play
   3. plans activities and lessons to help children move to next level
   4. recognizes that a child at cooperative level may want to play alone occasionally
B. Helps children respect the property and rights of others (through teacher's modeling of treatment of each child's property and rights; modeling behavior of teacher)
C. Helps children respect the personal feelings of others
D. Recognizes role of language in social development
E. Uses settling of disputes among children to demonstrate fairness and respect for others

*Outdoors*
A. Utilizes outdoor activities to their fullest extent as experiences for socialization (playground play, trips, walks, etc.)

X. Functional Area: *Guidance and Discipline*

*Indoors and Outdoors*
A. Allows for active and quiet periods (good scheduling of daily events)
B. Shares responsibility with other adults for planning and implementing activities of the group; shares information about children with other staff, encourages use of everyone's skills for benefit of children
C. Schedules activities in consideration of the needs of children; is flexible with scheduling
D. Understands need and plans for transition periods
E. Makes rules for health and safety of children; allows children to help make other rules
F. Understands reasons for and elements of group supervision

XI. Functional Area: *Families*

A. Establishes and promotes productive relationship with parents so as to increase the center's ability to help parents meet their child-rearing responsibilities

**FIGURE 8–3 cont'd.**

112

1. greets parents during arrival and departure times
2. attempts to share information about child with his or her parents
3. maintains an open ear to spoken and unspoken parental concerns
4. respects parents' need for involvement in child's school life
5. respects information parents have about their own child; seeks to obtain and use it

B. Provides opportunities for parents to use their skills and talents in the group
   1. attempts to identify parent skills
   2. finds ways to use the skills
C. Encourages participation in parent-advisory groups at the center

XII. Functional Area: *Program Management*

A. Makes written daily plans for the day's activities
   1. consults with other staff in preparation and evaluation activities
   2. uses community resources for program planning
   3. consults with parents regarding curriculum planning and encourages parental contribution
B. Keeps records appropriate to children and program
   1. uses appropriate techniques for observation and record keeping
   2. demonstrates awareness of situations/behaviors that should be recorded
   3. observes appropriate professional standards with regard to children's records and privileged information about families
C. Conducts regular evaluations of program
   1. requests input from co-workers regarding program activities
   2. accepts/seeks input from parents regarding program
   3. seeks/accepts input from the community regarding the program

XIII. Functional Area: *Professionalism*

A. Plans activities with other adults working with the group
   1. uses staff meetings
   2. shares information learned in classes, workshops
   3. seeks out staff with special skills for certain projects
   4. respects individual staff members' areas of expertise
B. Records pertinent information about children in the group
   1. shares this with staff
   2. recognizes staff roles in handling children's problems
C. Attends workshops, seminars, etc., when possible
   1. considers other staff members in planning time away from the center and in bringing back information

**FIGURE 8–3 cont'd.**

## OBSERVATION FORM

Suggestions for use of the *Observation Form:*

A. Advise staff of plans to observe and the purpose.
B. Observer should familiarize self with form items before beginning observation.
C. Observe for only one category of competence at a time.
   We suggest a short observation period of no more than 30 minutes.
D. Observe staff members at various times of day.
E. Avoid conducting several observations of the same person on consecutive days.
F. Keep in mind the extent of each staff member's authority and responsibility.
G. Record observations immediately.

**Safe**  Yes  No

1. Shows children correct way to handle scissors (how to pass, carry, etc.) _____ _____

2. Posts fire-drill regulations _____ _____

3. Reminds children of safety rules on walks, e.g., keep away from curb, red light means stop, no running, etc. _____ _____

4. Reminds children of classroom rules, e.g., no running, no pushing, etc. _____ _____

5. Checks that rules are in evidence on the playground and in the gym _____ _____

6. Makes sure that emergency contacts list is available _____ _____

7. Ascertains that list of emergency treatments or other first-aid information is readily available _____ _____

8. Ensures that large equipment is sturdy and free from sharp edges _____ _____

9. Stations self so can see all areas of classroom _____ _____

10. Notices potential danger and advises children, e.g., "Watch the custodian's bucket." _____ _____

11. Checks that first-aid kit is available in the room _____ _____

12. Sees to it that light and ventilation are regulated _____ _____

**Healthy**

1. Reminds child to use tissues as needed _____ _____

2. Reminds child to wash and dry hands carefully; models as needed _____ _____

3. Assures that each child has a change of clothes _____ _____

4. Checks that children brush teeth _____ _____

**FIGURE 8–4**

|  | Yes | No |
|---|---|---|

5. Provides children's books on health-related issues    \_\_\_\_\_   \_\_\_\_\_

6. Makes sure children are dressed for weather, e.g., zippered up in cold weather; allowed to remove sweaters if too warm    \_\_\_\_\_   \_\_\_\_\_

7. Teaches children proper toileting procedures    \_\_\_\_\_   \_\_\_\_\_

8. Ascertains that bathrooms are well supplied with soap, towels, tissues    \_\_\_\_\_   \_\_\_\_\_

9. Mentions food and its importance during the day    \_\_\_\_\_   \_\_\_\_\_

10. Reminds child to cover mouth when coughing or sneezing; models as needed    \_\_\_\_\_   \_\_\_\_\_

11. Models by eating at least some of all food served    \_\_\_\_\_   \_\_\_\_\_

12. Checks that cots are individually labeled with children's names    \_\_\_\_\_   \_\_\_\_\_

## Learning Environment

1. Encourages use of recognizable interest areas in room    \_\_\_\_\_   \_\_\_\_\_

2. Makes sure that interest areas have a variety of equipment, e.g., utensils, food props, pots/pans in kitchen area    \_\_\_\_\_   \_\_\_\_\_

3. Sees that materials are kept in order on shelves    \_\_\_\_\_   \_\_\_\_\_

4. Checks that materials are within child's reach    \_\_\_\_\_   \_\_\_\_\_

5. Sees to it that materials are in good condition and games complete; repairs in evidence are carefully done    \_\_\_\_\_   \_\_\_\_\_

6. Assures that materials are sufficient to provide challenge and variety for the age and ability of the group being taught in terms of social, emotional, physical, and intellectual development    \_\_\_\_\_   \_\_\_\_\_

7. Sees to it that there is an overall sense of order in the environment; care is evidenced in the arrangement of wall displays, furniture, and individual areas    \_\_\_\_\_   \_\_\_\_\_

8. Makes sure that wall displays are at child's eye level    \_\_\_\_\_   \_\_\_\_\_

9. Assures that room arrangement provides for smooth movement for adults and children, but is not such as to encourage excessive, uncontrolled running    \_\_\_\_\_   \_\_\_\_\_

10. Knows that wall displays and/or materials reflect awareness of children's cultural identity    \_\_\_\_\_   \_\_\_\_\_

11. Sees to it that outdoor area is available for gross-motor play    \_\_\_\_\_   \_\_\_\_\_

12. Checks that materials for gross-motor play are available indoors and outside    \_\_\_\_\_   \_\_\_\_\_

**FIGURE 8–4 cont'd.**

## Physical

| | Yes | No |
|---|---|---|
| 1. Makes sure that children engage in at least two specific fine-motor activities during the day, e.g., scissor cutting, collage, bead stringing | ____ | ____ |
| 2. Encourages the children to use two or more of their senses informally or through planned lesson or activity | ____ | ____ |
| 3. Sees to it that children engage in at least two specific gross-motor activities, e.g., circle, line exercises, use of jungle gym, relay race, etc. | ____ | ____ |
| 4. Gives a specific lesson or demonstration on a fine-motor skill | ____ | ____ |
| 5. Gives a specific lesson or demonstration on a gross-motor skill | ____ | ____ |
| 6. Checks that the following fine-motor-related materials are in evidence within room: scissors, paste and collage, beads and string, small Legos or building blocks, easel and paints, clay, puzzles | ____ | ____ |
| 7. Makes sure that the following gross motor-related materials are in evidence within the center and/or outdoor play area: large clocks, climbing apparatus, balancing beam or floor tape, riding/pushing toys | ____ | ____ |
| 8. Assures that gross motor play period is in part structured through either the use of equipment sufficient to the number and skill of the group, and/or through the use of group games | ____ | ____ |
| 9. Urges children to participate in some gross-motor activity during the day | ____ | ____ |
| 10. Implements activities that demonstrate an interrelationship of physical development with the disciplines, i.e., marching to music or food preparation (cutting and chopping vegetables) as a social activity | ____ | ____ |
| 11. Provides indoor as well as outdoor opportunities and spaces for gross-motor development | ____ | ____ |
| 12. Evidences planning for motor activities, as opposed to allowing them to occur at random | ____ | ____ |

## Cognitive

| | Yes | No |
|---|---|---|
| 1. Sees to it that pre-math materials are in evidence, e.g., peg board, geo board | ____ | ____ |
| 2. Assures that math materials are in evidence, e.g., numbers and pegs, sandpaper or rubber inset numbers | ____ | ____ |
| 3. Makes sure that science materials are available, e.g., magnifying glass, plants, living animals, collections of rocks, shells, leaves, moss, pine cones | ____ | ____ |

**FIGURE 8–4 cont'd.**

|  | Yes | No |
|---|---|---|

4. Urges that children engage in at least two cognitive activities, e.g., sorting, counting, matching, etc. _____ _____

5. Makes at least two interventions regarding the foregoing activities related to helping the child understand the cognitive concepts involved, e.g., "You sorted the beads into two piles. These are all red and these are all blue," or "Can you sort these into two different piles?" _____ _____

6. Asks informal questions or makes observations frequently throughout the day that encourage cognitive development, e.g., "We have two kinds of vegetables today, broccoli and corn," or "Can you think of how we could make pink paint?" _____ _____

7. Plans and conducts classifying or counting or grouping activities outdoors _____ _____

8. Refers to the time when mentioning upcoming activities, i.e., "It is ten o'clock and time for circle," in order to develop time concepts _____ _____

9. Creates problem-solving opportunities for children, i.e., "Why do you think this plant died and this one is so green?" _____ _____

10. Helps children to develop senses, i.e., "How does this feel?" or "How does that smell?" or "Is the taste sweet or sour?" _____ _____

11. Creates opportunities for children to develop observation skills, i.e., "Let's watch to see how much our plants grow. We can measure them and write down how tall they are." _____ _____

12. Urges children to make comparisons and contrasts between objects, colors, human characteristics, etc. _____ _____

## Communication

1. Encourages verbal expression at snack, lunch, and circle time, e.g., "Tell me what you did this morning." _____ _____

2. Listens attentively _____ _____

3. Provides books of various kinds _____ _____

4. Reads books to the group _____ _____

5. Speaks clearly and distinctly, modeling appropriate language _____ _____

6. Encourages vocabulary development by expressing complete rather than shorthand thoughts, e.g., "Please bring me the red ball from under the hexagonal table," rather than "Bring it here." _____ _____

7. Mirrors the child's speech in grammatically correct form, e.g., the child says during the child's lotto game "Who gots the bakery?" Teacher responds, "Who has the bakery? I have the bakery." _____ _____

**FIGURE 8–4 cont'd.**

|  | Yes | No |
|---|---|---|

8. Extends children's speech, e.g., teacher might add to the above response "The baker is in the window of the bakery." _____ _____

9. Helps the child make the connection between the spoken and written word through display of printed signs and labels _____ _____

10. Occasionally uses difficult words or phrases to extend child's receptive vocabulary _____ _____

11. Provides reinforcement for appropriate speech, new vocabulary _____ _____

12. Models good manners and respect for individual children through speech _____ _____

## Creative

1. Assures that materials are in evidence for use in creative expression, e.g., housekeeping area with related equipment utensils, food props, dolls, doll clothes, children's dress-ups, blocks of assorted kinds, sand table, puppets, art supplies, musical instruments _____ _____

2. Displays creative work of children _____ _____

3. Makes comments which extend the creative experience, e.g., "You've made a bridge. Do I need to pay a toll to cross over?" _____ _____

4. Encourages individual imagination, e.g., "I made my building look the way I want it. Make yours to look the way you want it to." _____ _____

5. Praises creative work _____ _____

6. Makes comments on work that helps the children notice particular, unique aspects of their work, e.g., "I like the colors that you choose." _____ _____

7. Avoids requiring the child to label creative work by asking "What is this?" but encourages free expression through open-ended questions, e.g., "Can you tell me about it?" _____ _____

8. Has art materials available and easily accessible to children: paper, paint, crayons, paste, collage materials, etc. _____ _____

9. Provides verbal reinforcement for a variety of children's creative efforts, such as "You look very nice today," or "I like the block city you built." _____ _____

10. Creates opportunities for creativity when children are outdoors, i.e., "Let's build sand castles in the sandbox," or "Can you make a design with those stones?" _____ _____

**FIGURE 8–4 cont'd.**

|  | Yes | No |
|---|---|---|

11. Helps children to use music as a tool for self-expression, i.e., "How does the music make you feel? Why don't you dance to show me?" _____ _____

12. Creates opportunities for dramatic outlets for children's feelings and ideas, i.e., "Show me how the wolf growled at Red Riding Hood," or "Let's tell the story of the 'wild things' without the book." _____ _____

**Self**

1. Greets each child by name on arrival _____ _____

2. Acknowledges children in positive ways for reasons other than group management _____ _____

3. Interacts with the children involved as individuals when a behavior problem arises and refrains from labeling children _____ _____

4. Maintains eye contact with children when talking and listening to them _____ _____

5. Attempts to sit, bend, or kneel so as to be on level with children _____ _____

6. Displays respectful behavior toward each child, e.g., uses please, thank you, etc.; refrains from unnecessary and abrupt interruptions into children's conversation or work _____ _____

7. Posts picture representation of the cultural ethnic groups to which the children belong _____ _____

8. Provides at least one activity or lesson that encourages sense of body awareness, e.g., body awareness cards, palm/foot prints, description of aspects of appearance, body outlines, silhouettes, photo of each child on display _____ _____

9. Encourages the child when helping him or her to practice so that child will learn the task alone, e.g., "There! I bet next time you'll be able to do it yourself." _____ _____

10. Provides ways to enable children to do as much as possible on their own, e.g., small brooms for sweeping, step-up in front of sink so child can adjust water easily, use of small pitchers or handles for quart-size containers so children can pour liquids themselves _____ _____

11. Looks for as many ways as possible for children to exercise responsibility, e.g., children may be encouraged to carry messages, help another child with a difficulty, scrape and stack dishes, clean up after meals and activities, water plants, feed pets, and use record or tape player alone _____ _____

**FIGURE 8–4 cont'd.**

|  | Yes | No |
|---|---|---|

12. Verbally conveys to the child that his or her jobs are important, e.g., "Thank you, Richard, for helping me sweep. I really needed help," or "You've set the table for us so now we may have a snack." _____ _____

13. Helps the child handle negative emotions in an appropriate way, e.g., "I know you're angry but I can't let you hit Johnny. Can you tell him that you didn't like what he did and that you're angry?" _____ _____

## Social

1. Greets each child upon arrival _____ _____

2. Helps the withdrawn newcomer by inviting him or her to join the group _____ _____

3. Shows awareness of the quiet, withdrawn child throughout the day through conversation and physical contact _____ _____

4. Takes advantage of opportunities to socially involve the withdrawn child, e.g., "Let's call Tamika over to join us." _____ _____

5. Sets an example for children to model, e.g., shows concern for another's feelings: "I know that cut must hurt you very much," or "Regina's not here today. I hope she's not too sick." _____ _____

6. Encourages children to empathize "How would you feel if someone didn't want you to play with them?" _____ _____

7. Encourages children to comfort others, e.g., "Jamila seems very sad today. Can you comfort her?" _____ _____

8. Encourages sense of community, e.g., "Let's wait for Derek to finish so he can join us." _____ _____

9. Teaches and reinforces socially acceptable behavior, i.e., table behavior, manners _____ _____

10. Helps children learn to share by providing activities that encourage this, e.g., use of a common bead container, collecting small pieces of clay from other children to provide for a new participant _____ _____

11. Helps children learn to take turns by providing turn-taking activities, e.g., having show and tell, playing group games like London Bridge _____ _____

12. Utilizes meal and snack times to encourage friendly discussion and sharing among children _____ _____

## Guidance and Discipline

1. Alternates quiet and active routines _____ _____

2. Provides quiet period, e.g., story or song before lunch as a transition period _____ _____

**FIGURE 8–4 cont'd.**

|  | Yes | No |
|---|---|---|

3. Provides complete coverage of the children by stationing co-workers in separate areas of room _____ _____

4. Shares advice and consults with co-workers, e.g., regarding changes in schedule _____ _____

5. Makes sure reminders of rules are in evidence to guide children's behavior, e.g., "Remember to walk." "Use your inside voices." _____ _____

6. Gives clear, consistent, and complete directions during transition periods, e.g., "When you finish putting all the toys away you may line up at the cubbies to go to the bathroom." _____ _____

7. Gives advance notice of end of period, e.g., "In five minutes we will clean up." _____ _____

8. Effectively sets limits and advises children of the consequences, e.g., "You may not hit anyone. If you hit David again you will have to leave the circle." _____ _____

9. Establishes external controls through the environment, e.g., class is divided into areas that limit running and chaotic movement _____ _____

10. Uses established areas for circle time; uses tape, mats, or rules for how to gather in the group _____ _____

11. Ignores minor attention-getting disruptions, e.g., a very bright child raises his or her hand to indicate that each name card displayed is that child's; teacher ignores this behavior _____ _____

12. Notices and commends positive behavior, e.g., "I like the way Akiba is sitting." _____ _____

**Families**

1. Greets parents by name as they drop off and pick up children _____ _____

2. Has a set of clean clothes for each child and reminds parents to replenish these as necessary _____ _____

3. Has phone numbers and emergency contacts available for each child _____ _____

4. Helps the child bridge the gap between home and school by asking questions and listening to stories, such as those about the home experiences of the child _____ _____

5. Limits children's use of overly personal conversation that is not necessary for teacher to hear in order to deal with the child's feelings _____ _____

6. Does not pump child for information but listens to and encourages child's expression of feelings _____ _____

**FIGURE 8–4 cont'd.**

|  | Yes | No |
|---|---|---|

7. Observes the child for changes in behavior and discusses these with parents _____ _____

8. Schedules parent conferences to formally discuss child's progress with parents _____ _____

9. Encourages observation by parents and their participation on class trips, visitation to share meals, or to teach a lesson or help in class _____ _____

10. Provides parents with techniques they may use at home to help children's development, e.g., encourages reading to the children, gives suggestions for appropriate Christmas toys, books, etc. _____ _____

11. Helps parents and child separate upon arrival at school by greeting the child and helping him or her become involved in a class activity _____ _____

12. Sees to it that parent bulletin board is evident and utilized _____ _____

**Program Management**

1. Plans with co-workers for centerwide trips, celebrations, center procedures _____ _____

2. Attends workshops and reports back to rest of staff either formally or informally _____ _____

3. Brings new ideas from college class and shares these with other staff _____ _____

4. Utilizes a structured format for recording observations of children's behaviors _____ _____

5. Develops and utilizes a plan for daily classroom activities _____ _____

6. Utilizes the skills and expertise of both co-workers and parents to plan the school program _____ _____

7. Keeps records of each child's physical, cognitive, and social development, utilizing these for daily individual planning _____ _____

8. Conducts regular evaluations of classroom activities and uses outcomes for program modification _____ _____

9. Uses community resources for program planning and implementation of children's program _____ _____

10. Discusses children's unusual behaviors or problems with co-workers and appropriate resource staff _____ _____

11. Accepts suggestions of co-workers, parents, board members regarding children's programs _____ _____

FIGURE 8–4 cont'd.

| | Yes | No |
|---|---|---|

12. Demonstrates flexibility, rather than rigidity with regard to the daily schedule, when circumstances indicate this is appropriate, i.e., making a schedule change when weather indicates that scheduled work is impossible          \_\_\_\_\_   \_\_\_\_\_

**Professionalism**

1. Is generally on time for work          \_\_\_\_\_   \_\_\_\_\_

2. Is generally present; avoids unnecessary absences          \_\_\_\_\_   \_\_\_\_\_

3. Assumes responsibility for all the children when several classes are at the playground, on trips, in the gym, etc. Avoids comments such as, "It isn't my job."          \_\_\_\_\_   \_\_\_\_\_

4. Assists other classes when there is staff shortage          \_\_\_\_\_   \_\_\_\_\_

5. Is courteous to other adults, especially in the presence of children          \_\_\_\_\_   \_\_\_\_\_

6. Avoids discussion of in-house matters in front of children and parents          \_\_\_\_\_   \_\_\_\_\_

7. Uses appropriate channels to settle disputes and avoids unnecessary discussion of these outside channels          \_\_\_\_\_   \_\_\_\_\_

8. Volunteers to assist with special center projects          \_\_\_\_\_   \_\_\_\_\_

9. Avoids open criticism of co-workers or director; demonstrates loyalty          \_\_\_\_\_   \_\_\_\_\_

10. Attends professional conferences of training when possible          \_\_\_\_\_   \_\_\_\_\_

11. Subscribes to professional magazines and journals and shares ideas with co-workers          \_\_\_\_\_   \_\_\_\_\_

12. Indicates ability to self-evaluate. Shows understanding of own strengths and weaknesses, i.e., "I would like to learn more activities for math skills development."          \_\_\_\_\_   \_\_\_\_\_

**FIGURE 8–4 cont'd.**

measuring a learner's integration and practical application of knowledge, these tools may be better measures of test-taking ability.

3. The assessment model of training, according to Goldsmith, should also have its basis in the social and cultural "realities" faced by the caregiver/learner and the client served. The early childhood professional copes with a lack of public recognition of the expertise required to function in the teaching/caregiving roles, accepts a degree of confusion regarding the paradigms of the field, and recognizes the tumultuous social changes now affecting parents and children. All of these factors influence the competencies essential for high-quality caregiving.

4. There may be, in some quarters, the mistaken belief that competency-based training approaches focus primarily on the practical. This is probably an accurate picture of some programs. But, as Goldsmith points out, this is an inappropriate direction for training to take. The content of assessment models, particularly those for early childhood educators, should focus upon instilling an understanding of the theoretical bases for practice. Caregivers must comprehend the reasons behind the curriculum developed, the equipment and materials utilized, and the interactions appropriate between adults and young children.

5. Yet another requirement for quality assessment-based programs is that these should result in an improvement of the services that caregivers provide for children and parents. In the experience of the authors, these programs may tend to be focused upon the increased status of the learner. This is a positive result of training. However, if the trainer and learners deemphasize the value of the assessment model as a tool for strengthening the caregiver's ability to recognize and respond to client needs, the program suffers.

6. As previously discussed in relation to the Child Development Associate Credential Award System, the assessment of competence should not be viewed as the end of the learning process. Some means must be devised to suggest to the learner those areas where further growth can occur. As a result of training, avenues must be opened up that provide directions toward new levels of professionalism for the caregiver.

In discussing these aspects of competency-based staff-development programs, we do not wish to infer that these are the only criteria. The very nature of the assessment process suggests that it must be highly individualized. Learning styles are always unique. Even when an entire group needs to learn the same skill, that need is individualized by the previous experiences (academic and professional), ability to conceptualize, and other aptitudes of each staff member. Roles of various personnel also determine their responsibilities and the skills required to function in their positions.

The designer of an assessment model system of training must be a skilled developer of instructional objectives, able to discern the critical skills of the caregiver and support staff. Knowing what child-care personnel should be able to demonstrate is, however, only one part of the training program. The second, equally important, task is the one of devising the appropriate training curriculum. Figure 8–5 contains descriptions of the Philadelphia Child Development Associate Training Program. It clearly illustrates the connection between training content and the competencies to be developed.

If proper consideration is given of the key factors in the competency-based training model, a director can be most successful in promoting staff growth, individual self-esteem and job satisfaction, and ultimately a higher-quality program.

## Advantages of Competency-Based Models

Strong proponents of assessment-based systems of training[8] point out that goals of this type of training are specified in advance, and both the trainers and learners can be held accountable for promotion and achievement of the desired outcomes.

The individualized and self-paced nature of this approach are not guarantees of success, but they do increase the chances that learners will achieve success by providing needed attention to the various means through which each person absorbs information.

Competency-based staff development models are also a systematic means of training early childhood personnel. Although trainers are well meaning, the approaches taken to information sharing or skills building are often somewhat haphazard. Insufficient time goes into a breakdown of factors influencing skills development, appropriate curriculum, or measurement of competencies attained. An assessment system mandates that all of these factors be given due consideration.

Finally, in this time of consumer awareness and a strong emphasis on accountability, the public is reassured and helped to regain some of the lost confidence in education when teacher competence can clearly be established.

## Criticisms of Competency-Based Training

Many of the concerns of the opponents of competency-based education[9] can be addressed through appropriate planning and understanding of the role of performance-based assessment. For example, while assessment of mastery activities should ideally occur at the site of the caregiver's work with children and performance should be the measure of competence, mastery activities should be designed to enable learners to demonstrate their integration of theory and practice. If demonstration of only practical skills is required, then only minimal levels of performance may be evidenced and special talents may go unrecognized.

Another concern of those who object to competency-based training is one related to the message that may inadvertently be conveyed when assessment is

## CHILD DEVELOPMENT ASSOCIATE TRAINING PROGRAM[10]
### (Sample Curriculum Content and Mastery Activities
### Based Upon The Seven Units and Twenty-One Modules in the Program)

| Unit Topic | Description of Unit Content | Sample Mastery Activity Description |
|---|---|---|
| I. Health and safety for young children | • State day-care regulations for health and safety<br>• Environmental conditions of classroom promoting health and safety<br>• First aid for injuries<br>• Basic nutrition<br>• Working with children with physical and mental health impairments | • Set up and maintain a health history folder describing the family history; birth circumstances; and physical, cognitive, social, and emotional development of a child in caregiver's classroom |
| II. Developing cognitive skills in young children | • Normal language development from birth to age five<br>• Growth of cognitive skills in preschool child<br>• Development of math and science skills<br>• Component of social studies education for preschool | • Develop and implement lesson plans for language arts, math, science, social studies |
| III. Caregiver social/ interpersonal skills | • Developing listening, responding, and other interactional skills<br>• Observing and recording children's behavior | • Select a child with some problem behavior: observe and record child's behavior; discuss with child his or her inappropriate behavior; develop a plan for promoting child's appropriate behavior |
| IV. Promoting caregiver's professional growth | • History of early childhood education and day-care movement | • Develop a personal plan for continuing professional development |

Reprinted by permission.

FIGURE 8–5

the end-of-the-road evaluation process. It is certainly true of the graduates of many traditional college programs that degree receipt is seen as the completion of the learning process. When competency assessment appears to be the final measure of achievement, the learner may mistakenly believe that a pinnacle of professional growth has been reached, and little or nothing more is necessary. As Joan Goldsmith has suggested, initiative to pursue lifelong learning must be promoted.

Those in the liberal arts have argued that this training approach neglects both educational foundations and the broad base in the humanities considered to be essential to high-quality teaching. In some competency-based programs, this might well be a justified criticism. If, however, caregivers are provided with the basic information relevant to child development (developmental psychology), family structure and interactions (sociology), social studies curriculum (history), science and mathematics curriculum, and creative expression (art history, music appreciation, and dramatics) the child care workers have a much more rounded educational experience than imagined by those critical members of the liberal arts community. Nonetheless, it is incumbent upon those who receive performance-based training to pursue additional experiences that truly round out their education.

Competency-based training and other staff development programs can be an alternative method, another direction for leaders in early childhood education who are concerned with the overall growth of the profession. Most important, therein lies one of the means for individuals to reach toward their potential and achieve the satisfaction gained when new abilities and contributions to the profession are self-evident.

## RECOMMENDED READING

Beaty, J. *Skills for Preschool Teachers*, Second Edition. Columbus, OH: Charles E. Merrill Publishing Company, 1984.

Beaty, J. *Teacher Competencies for Preschool Programs: A Self-Study Guide to CDA Assessment.* Elmira, NY: 3 to 5 (P.O. Box 3213, 14905), 1981.

Blake, M. E. (ed.). *Day Care Aides: A Guide for Inservice Training,* Second Edition. New York: National Federation of Settlements and Neighborhood Centers, 1972.

Blank, W. E. *Handbook for Developing Competency-Based Training Programs.* Englewood Cliffs, NJ: Prentice-Hall, Inc., 1982.

Conger, F. S., and I. B. Rose. *Child Care Aide Skills.* New York: McGraw-Hill Book Company, 1979.

Houston, W. R., and R. B. Howsam. *Competency-Based Teacher Education.* Chicago: Science Research Associates, Inc., 1972.

Kasindorf, M. E. *Competencies: A Self-Guide in Early Childhood Education.* Atlanta, GA: Humanics Limited, 1980.

Mager, R. F. *Preparing Instructional Objectives*, Second Edition. Belmont, CA: Fearon-Pitman Publishers, Inc., 1975.

McAsham, H. H. *Competency-Based Education and Behavioral Objectives*. Englewood Cliffs, NJ: Educational Technology Publishers, 1979.

*Performance-Based Teacher Education Series*. Washington, DC: American Association of Colleges for Teacher Education.

Yelon, S. L., and J. S. Duley. *Efficient Evaluation of Individual Performance in Field Placement*, Guides for the Improvement of Instruction in Higher Education, No. 14. East Lansing, MI: Michigan State University, 1978.

## CHAPTER 8 NOTES

1. Joan Goldsmith, "Competence Assessment Within a Professional Training Program," in P. S. Pottinger and J. Goldsmith (eds.), *Designing and Measuring Competence*. San Francisco: Jossey-Bass Inc., Publishers, 1979.

2. J. M. Rich, "Competency/Performance—Band Teacher Education," *Innovation in Education: Reformers and Their Critics*, Second Edition. Boston: Allyn and Bacon, Inc., 1978, pp. 212–213.

3. Leroy Jones et al. *The Child Development Associate Program: A Guide to Program Administration*. Washington, DC: U.S. Department of Health and Human Services, Office of Human Development Services, Administration for Children, Youth and Families, Head Start Bureau, 1981, pp. 2–3.

4. Ibid.

5. E. A. Brawley et al. "A Competency-Based Training Program for Day Care Personnel," *Child Care Quarterly*, Vol. 10, No. 2, Summer 1981, pp. 125–136.

6. *CDA Candidate's Local Assessment Team Book*. Washington, DC: U.S. Department of Health and Human Services, Office of Human Development Services, Administration for Children, Youth, and Families, Head Start Bureau, 1981.

7. Goldsmith, pp. 53–63.

8. J. M. Rich, ibid.

9. Ibid.

10. *The Child Development Associate Training Program*. Philadelphia: Community College of Philadelphia, Research for Better Schools, The School District of Philadelphia, 1974.

# CHAPTER 9

# Training Parents and Other Volunteer Staff

ONE OF THE greatest assets of an early childhood program is a strong volunteer program. Economic and social factors, reacting on programs for young children, have made the process of adequately staffing programs a complicated responsibility of directors. Budgets of federally funded programs have been considerably tightened. Maintaining the energy and enthusiasm of caregivers is to some extent dependent upon the assurance that vacation time and sick and personal leave days may be taken as needed, without imposing hardship on co-workers. Unfortunately, many centers receiving government grants have all but lost monies for substitute staff.

The quality of curriculum is also affected by staffing problems. For example, when fewer adults are in the classroom, much of the day may be taken up by caregiving routines. This is a special problem when infants and pre-schoolers are the clients. Changing, feeding, toileting, hand washing, dressing and undressing for outdoor activities can consume large amounts of time. Individualized attention may be almost impossible. Little time may be left for other learning activities when a classroom is short of caregivers. Field trips, neighborhood walks, and other experiences beneficial to children may be impossible to implement without extra hands and eyes. This is where volunteer workers can be invaluable.

The advantages of a strong volunteer component are, however, more than just practical in nature. Whether parents or helpers from the community, the presence of volunteers can create a special awareness among employed personnel. Staff may be helped to see themselves as representatives of the early childhood profession, from whom the community gets its picture of the teaching and caregiving roles. When parents are volunteers, staff have opportunities to observe them in their interactions with their children and the children of others. Furthermore, having parent volunteers is one of the best ways to familiarize families with the philosophy, goals, and curriculum of a program. Not only do the volunteers get the message, but they are often instrumental in spreading it to other parents.

Volunteers from home and community often bring fresh, untried points of view to an early childhood program. After all, those who volunteer their services often do so for love of the work—in this case, love of children. Working with youngsters for the first time is usually an exciting experience, full of discoveries about the nature, development, and behavior of children. Volunteers can help early childhood staff acquire a renewed awareness of those feelings that brought them to the profession.

This chapter will focus not only on the many benefits of developing a volunteer program, but also on the processes of orienting, training, and evaluating a range of volunteer workers.

## PARENT VOLUNTEERS

Among the many parent involvement avenues available to child-care and school programs is that of the solicitation and utilization of parent volunteers.* It is not an uncommon practice for parents to work in the unpaid capacities of classroom, noontime, or field-trip aides to teachers. There are, however, ways to design and implement a parent involvement program that are likely to promote its success.

Without appearing to be pessimistic, an important starting point for the entire parent involvement component is an exploration of the realities of home-school relationships.

First, not all teachers welcome parents into the classroom. Some have had unpleasant past interactions with mothers or fathers. Some teachers doubt the contributions parents can make, feeling that expertise in child development should be a prerequisite to classroom involvement. Still others who staff classrooms feel that parents are scrutinizing their interactions with children and may find fault with teaching practices.

A second reality of parent involvement programs is that not all parents are suited to all forms of school volunteer work. Certain interpersonal skills, some self-direction, and the ability to separate self from one's own child are among the qualities of a classroom aide. Problems can develop when a parent attempts to usurp the authority of the teacher or in other ways misinterprets the volunteer role. A problem frequently observed by the authors is that one referred to by Berger when she addresses five kinds of common responses that parents have to school.[1] She suggests that some individuals develop an attachment to the power that can evolve out of overinvolvement at school. While a certain level of involvement is important for all families, too strong a parent leadership role can have the negative effect of keeping other parents away. Others may have the impression that there is no place for them at school. The authors have observed this message very effectively delivered by those parents attempting to assert their powerful positions at school.

A director must be a keen judge of character and on top of volunteer activity at all times. When a strong-willed person takes the helm of coordinator of parent involvement activity, some school administrators may mistakenly believe that they can relax and let that parent run this particular component of

---

*Because this volume deals with staff and volunteer roles, this chapter will not contain information on other parent-involvement activities. The authors acknowledge the need for many other roles for working parents who wish to be involved in their youngsters' programs.

the program. This can be a serious mistake, which ultimately undermines the program and may drive potential volunteers away. A program should have room for many parent volunteers in a variety of leadership roles.

## Promoting Parent Volunteerism

Having explored factors that can impede all forms of parent involvement, we now wish to discuss the processes for instituting an effective volunteer program for parents. One of the first steps a school administrator can take relates to one of the home-school realities previously discussed. A director must be aware of the perspectives of staff regarding parents. Knowing how caregivers and support staff feel about parents, both individually and as a group, is critical information to have before enlisting parent volunteers.

Equally important to the inquiry process is knowing the feelings of staff about family participation in the school program. At times, the program administrator must take specific steps to help facilitate attitudinal changes among caregivers before encouraging various roles of parents in school. A type of staff development may be essential to facilitate discussion of feelings about parents and open doors for new forms of interaction with them. One device for moving in this direction is suggested in Figure 9–1.

A sometimes neglected aspect of developing a parent volunteer program is that of learning the full extent of parents' talents, interests, and availability. Ideally, at the time of enrollment, parents should be provided with a question-naire (such as that shown in Figure 9–2) to help facilitate their degree of participation in the family-involvement program. Parents should know from the outset that there are many options for volunteerism, not merely that of classroom aide. (NOTE: A variation of Figure 9–2 can very easily be used as an application for all volunteers.)

Given the types of early childhood programs in question (day-care centers, nursery school, primary school, parent cooperative), the next of the steps to a strong parent-volunteer program is mapping out its parameters. What goals will the program have? In what capacities will parents function? Some suggestions for volunteer roles of parents include the following:

*Classroom Aides*

- Demonstrating talents or skills
- Discussing a trip/showing slides
- Tutoring children
- Playing games with children
- Helping children with skills practice activities
- Reading stories to children
- Supervising children's indoor/outdoor activities
- Making or collecting activity materials

## STAFF DEVELOPMENT ACTIVITY TO PROMOTE
## PARENT INVOLVEMENT

Directions for Group Facilitator: Have staff rate each of the following statements on a scale from one to five. One (1) indicates no approval of the statement, three (3) signifies some approval, five (5) is an indication of full approval of the statement. Following completion of the exercise, the staff as a group should discuss those items they agree and disagree on and the reasons. The group should also discuss those factors that would increase their ratings of each item.

1. Parents are very involved in the program at our center. _____

2. Parents are a great resource to our early childhood program. _____

3. Parents have many opportunities to contribute to our program. _____

4. Our staff works hard to make parents feel comfortable while at school. _____

5. Parents seem to understand the philosophy and goals of our program. _____

6. Parents are free to communicate their concerns about the program to staff. _____

7. Those parents who are concerned about their children come to school regularly. _____

8. Parents have a right to be upset or angry if they feel that they are not being heard by staff. _____

9. Parents are eager to learn, especially about their children. _____

10. Parents need training to do the best in their volunteer roles. _____

11. There are areas in which our parent involvement component could be improved. _____

12. I have a close working relationship with most of the parents of children in my classroom. _____

13. I enjoy working while parents are in the classroom. _____

14. I am familiar with the jobs and interests of the parents of children in my classroom. _____

15. I communicate at least once a month with parents of children in my classroom. _____

FIGURE 9–1

## PARENT INVOLVEMENT QUESTIONNAIRE

Dear Parent:

This questionnaire is designed to enable you to give input into the role you would like to play in our program. We would like to know the extent of your talents and interests and to familiarize you with all of the parent involvement possibilities and family activities going on at the Center. Thank you for your cooperation.

_____
Director

Your Name: _____ Child's Name: _____

Relationship to Child: _____

No. of Child's Siblings and Ages: _____

Address: _____

Home Telephone: _____

Job Title: _____

Employer: _____

Address: _____

Work Telephone: _____

Hours/Days Worked Per Week: _____

Hobbies: _____

Special Interests or Talents: _____

Musical Instruments Played: _____

Cities and Countries Traveled To: _____

_____

_____

_____

Armed Forces Service: _____

**FIGURE 9–2**

Check those activities you would like to participate in at the Center or at home. This does not mean you are committed to that activity.

| | |
|---|---|
| _____ Working as a classroom aide | _____ Contributing to center newsletter |
| _____ Accompanying the children on field trips | _____ Participating in the parent telephone tree |
| _____ Collecting materials for children's projects | _____ Collecting dress ups for dramatic play |
| _____ Helping prepare for holiday/ birthday parties | _____ Answering telephones in center office |
| _____ Preparing baked goods for fund-raising events | _____ Sending out mailings to parents, community |
| _____ Making special presentations to children (talking about your job, a trip, playing an instrument) | _____ Donating books to the center |
| | _____ Other (Please describe) |

Hours/Days you would be available for Center activities: _____

_____

Briefly describe what you most enjoy doing when you are with your child:

_____

_____

_____

_____

_____
Signature

_____
Date

© 1987 by The Center for Applied Research in Education, Inc.

**FIGURE 9–2 cont'd.**

*Nonteaching Aides at Center*

- Clerical work in school office
- Collecting fees from other parents
- Preparing home-school literature
- Serving on committees
- Serving on advisory board
- Editing a center newsletter
- Coordinating parent-education programs
- Coordinating volunteer program

*Volunteer-from-Home Projects*

- Coordinating telephone tree
- Baby sitting for others attending school events
- Collecting materials for school projects
- Preparing refreshments for school activities
- Repairing children's toys or games
- Sewing costumes or art aprons for children
- Telephoning for information about field trips
- Making name badges for field trips

It is essential that roles of parent volunteers be spelled out. Parents must be given not merely the names of the jobs that they will function in, but their specific responsibilities must be identified. During the orientation process, all volunteers should receive written information about the policies and procedures pertaining to them. It is difficult for persons to successfully function in roles that they do not understand. It is through the volunteer orientation and training processes that parents and others can be familiarized with the scope of their activities.

A final note on family involvement in early childhood programs. We have referred to parents as the persons who should be sought for volunteer participation. A much overlooked family resource are children's grandparents, aunts and uncles, and teenage siblings, who can also be active in programs for young children. Keeping the door open to all the members of the family can only be of benefit to the entire program.

## VOLUNTEERS FROM THE COMMUNITY

One of the keys to acquiring volunteers from the community is the involvement of the director with business leaders and a variety of local organizations. No matter the size of the community, large urban area to small town, each has a city council, Chamber of Commerce, and charitable organizations. As a program administrator, an early childhood director should be knowledgeable about all of the business and service groups in the community. The need for volunteers should be on the agenda of group meetings, along with the special concerns of each agency represented.

A surprising number of organizations exist for the purpose of identifying and responding to the needs in the community. Many of the volunteers and other needs of the early childhood center can be addressed by these groups. We suggest contacting the local chapters of these organizations and others to inquire about the availability of volunteer services.

Action Alliance of Senior Citizens
American Association of University Women
Benevolent Association of Elks
Big Brother/Big Sister Association of America
Boys/Girls Clubs of America
Boy Scouts/Girl Scouts of America
Daughters/Sons of the American Revolution
Foster Grandparents*
Gray Panthers*
Hearts and Hands Foundation for the Handicapped
Irish Society
Jewish Y's and Centers
Knights of Columbus
Lions Clubs

Masons
National Council of Jewish Women
Odd Fellows
Polish American Congress
Retired Police and Firemen
Retired Senior Volunteer Program*
Rotary Club
Russian Brotherhood Organization of U.S.A.
Salvation Army
Shriners
Sons of Italy
Urban League
Variety Club
Veterans Administration
Veterans of Foreign Wars
Volunteer Action Council
Women in Community Service, Inc.

*Refers to service organizations whose members are senior citizens.

All potential volunteers should be advised of the many benefits to be gained by this activity. Volunteering in an early childhood program is an opportunity to meet new people, learn new skills and information, gain experiences that may lead to employment, and contribute to the needs of children and families. In addition, any center seeking volunteers should consider offering transportation money, hot lunch and snacks, baby sitting, volunteer certificates, annual luncheons, and other ways of rewarding the special efforts of volunteer workers.

## Senior Volunteers

Mention has already been made of the possibility of enlisting grandparents as volunteers in early childhood programs. The foregoing list contains the names of several senior service organizations that are additional sources of older adult volunteers. We would like, however, to briefly discuss the reasons that seniors are so badly needed in programs for young children.

The structure of family life has changed significantly in the past fifty years. No longer are extended families as physically or, in some cases, as emotionally close as they once were. Kornhaber and Woodward have written about the impact of a "new social contract"[2] impacting on the lives of grandparents and grandchildren. In a world that values youth and independence, it is no longer fashionable to be a grandparent. Grandparents are being urged to value independence and noninvolvement in this new way of life, where "emotions equal weakness" and "intimacy equals emotional dependence."[3]

Perhaps the most unfortunate effect of the "new social contract" is its impact on children. While not parties to the contract, say Woodward and Kornhaber, children are the "primary victims" through their loss of the loving allies found in nurturing grandparents.[4] It is through grandparents that centuries of youngsters have learned the joys of intimate relationships and heard the stories passed down by the older generation. Many psychologists and sociologists believe that the long-term effects of being reared without the strong, positive influence of grandparents will not be minimal.

When seniors become volunteers in the early childhood setting, the potential exists for many benefits for children and parents. The youngsters have restored to them important and reassuring grandparent figures. Mothers and fathers, who have been deprived of the patience, understanding, and experience that can come with involvement by their own parents, may have a vital support system restored to them. To put it bluntly, young mothers and fathers sometimes need parenting themselves, a role that senior volunteers can fill.

Senior citizens have been given mixed messages by our society. It may be difficult for them to get or keep a job when they reach a certain age. They are forced into retirement, often before they are ready for it. They are expected to enjoy the "golden years," having moved over to make room for the younger generation. Families may be instrumental in urging seniors to sell the homes they have lived in for years that are now difficult for them to maintain in order to move into retirement communities. Many older people get both media and cultural messages that read, "You have earned your freedom from responsibility. Enjoy it." For some seniors, the impact of all of this is a sense of purposelessness. Their children do not need them; their grandchildren are in day care; their jobs have been taken by younger people.

Working with youngsters through the volunteer Foster Grandparents Program or another community service organization helps to ease the sense of loss experienced by many older adults. Young children have clear-cut needs that senior volunteers can see and respond to. Little ones also provide ears eager for the stories, adventures, and wisdom that develop with experience. While volunteering in early childhood education does not meet all of the needs of older adults, it can provide them with a renewed sense of purpose and belongingness.

## Working with Student Teachers

Local college and university programs can be a great source of supplementary staff for early childhood programs. Departments of early childhood education, child care, and child development, even psychology and nursing programs, often seek sites that will provide a practicum experience for their students.

Working with student learners, however, requires a somewhat different commitment on the part of the center staff. There will be a systematic program to be followed and specific skills to be developed by the student teacher. This individual, unlike other volunteers, is preparing to assume a professional role with children. Staff may need to complete forms recording the student's progress and meet on a regular basis with a representative of the college attended by the student.

For the cooperating teacher there is work, but there are also many rewards. The student teacher is actively involved in learning about children. The student can be the source of many new ways of looking at children's behavior and interacting with them. The process of evaluating practicum students can also provide staff with ways of looking at themselves and considering their own professional development.

We would urge those directors who are considering utilizing student teachers or who already have them working in the center to take into account the following suggestions from the authors based upon many years of supervising college students in early childhood settings:

- Many teachers/caregivers have an unclear conception of the cooperating-teacher role they must assume in relation to student teachers. This role must be clearly established by the center and the college before student teachers arrive at the center.

- The college must provide clearly stated systematic guidelines for the student's role. The progress expected from the student on a weekly basis should be spelled out, along with the measures to be used to evaluate skills growth.

- Not all staff are suited for the cooperating teacher role. These individuals must be role models for their student teachers. The ability to break down teaching tasks and techniques in order to explain or demonstrate them is essential. An effective cooperating teacher must be able to help the student identify strengths and weaknesses and work to maximize or overcome these.

- Cooperating teachers must be open to developing and maintaining communication with the college supervisor. These two individuals work together to plan for and evaluate the student's practicum program. Good communication skills are essential for these staff members.

With thought and effort the involvement of student teachers can be a rewarding experience for students and staff.

## VOLUNTEER ORIENTATION AND TRAINING

The goals of volunteer orientation are to describe the philosophy, policies, and purposes of the early childhood program; to describe the roles that volunteers can play; to help volunteers select a job and develop an understanding of what the related responsibilities are; and to familiarize volunteers with the staff, facility, and children. Orientation should be an occasion to convey to volunteers enthusiasm of those employed in the program, while emphasizing the value of the roles volunteers play.

While volunteers can be oriented singly, it gives a sense of support and comradery if several can be introduced to the program at the same time. It is also less taxing for those who conduct orientation if small group orientations are held. Sessions should be planned in advance of any other volunteer activity at the center, and consideration should be given to who will conduct orientation, when and where it will be held, and what materials and activities will be presented. Figure 9–3 provides a sample agenda for a volunteer orientation workshop.

### Training for Volunteers

Orientation should be only a first step in the volunteer education process. Most, although not all, volunteer roles require additional information and skills development over time. Particularly when roles involve direct service to children and parents, an ongoing volunteer training program should be instituted. The authors have found that it is not always necessary to separate staff (paid employees in some sessions, volunteers attending others). In fact, it may contribute significantly to team and partnership feelings when all staff participate in the same training.

There are, however, some topics of special interest and concern to volunteers, especially when they have had no previous classroom experience with young children. Some recommended training topics for volunteers are:

1. Child Development
2. Behavior Management
3. Child Health and Safety
4. Working with Children Individually and in Groups
5. Games and Songs for Young Children

## VOLUNTEER ORIENTATION WORKSHOP AGENDA

I. Welcome
  A. Introduction of center staff
II. The volunteer program
  A. Word of appreciation to volunteers
  B. Goals of volunteer program
  C. Benefits of volunteer activity to children, parents, staff, overall center program

III. About the center
  A. Philosophy and goals
  B. Policies and procedures (handbooks should be provided)
  C. Description of program
    1. Number of classrooms, children in care, ages (provide floor plan of center)
    2. Description of curriculum, daily schedule
    3. Office activities
    4. Nutrition component
    5. Involvement with parents and community
    6. Other components

IV. Roles of volunteers
  A. Special need for volunteer staff
  B. Description of available jobs for volunteers
    1. Responsibilities
    2. Hours needed
  C. Additional training available

V. Questions and answers

VI. Scheduling of volunteers

FIGURE 9–3

## GUIDELINES FOR VOLUNTEERS
## GRANT CHILD DEVELOPMENT CENTER

1. Remember to sign in when you arrive at the center and sign out when you leave.

2. Telephone the center if you will be late or unable to attend on a given day. Call in advance, if possible. Remember, we count on you.

3. Consult the daily schedule posted in the office or classroom where you are assigned. Discuss any questions about the day's events or your role in them with a staff member.

4. Please treat all information encountered related to children and their families confidentially.

5. If a problem related to your work develops, feel free to discuss the matter with the director.

6. Refer parents, relatives of children, and other visitors with questions to the classroom teacher or the office.

7. Let the director or classroom teacher know of your suggestions or ideas for improving the program.

8. Please dress comfortably for work with the children. Avoid high heels, brief skirts, shorts (pants), or halter tops.

9. Refer serious discipline problems to the classroom teacher. Refrain from corporal punishment at all times.

10. Never leave children unattended.

Thank you for your efforts on behalf of our program!


Yvette Monroe
Director


FIGURE 9–4

The volunteers knowing that they are considered part of the team, that they are given opportunities for input and are not merely used to accomplish the jobs that no one else wants contributes measurably to the success of these programs.

Volunteers need also to be given a set of guidelines for school procedures. A copy of these guidelines (see the sample in Figure 9–4) can be given to each volunteer.

## Evaluating Volunteer Services

On a regular and ongoing basis, assessment should be made of the volunteer component and individual volunteers. It is important to know how well volunteers have adapted to the program and what impact their work has on children, parents, and staff. We recommend regular observation of volunteer workers and means for staff and parents to give feedback on their perceptions. Volunteers themselves should be asked to give input about the program. Chapter 11 contains additional information on evaluation procedures.

## Recognizing Volunteer Efforts

Volunteer services should not be taken for granted. Several times each year the director and staff should honor their volunteers with recognition ceremonies and awards. Hand-lettered certificates, gifts made by the children, coffee mugs with each volunteer's name (when other staff have them), a luncheon or dinner held in their honor are some ways of letting volunteers know their efforts are of value to everyone at the center. Even when people do not receive monetary compensation for their work, they need to know they are appreciated and make a contribution through their role in the program.

## RECOMMENDED READING

Brock, H. C. III. *Parent Volunteer Programs in Early Childhood Education: A Practical Guide.* Hamden, CT: Shoestring Press, 1976.

Chinn, P. C. et al. *Two-Way Talking with Parents of Special Children: A Process of Positive Communication.* St. Louis, MO: C. V. Mosby Company, 1978.

*Handbook for Teachers: Effective Involvement of School Volunteers.* Alexandria, VA: National School Volunteer Program, Inc., 1979.

Honig, A. S. *Parent Involvement in Early Childhood Education.* Washington, D.C.: National Association for the Education of Young Children, 1975.

Inglis, R. L. *A Time to Learn: A Guide for Parents to the New Theories in Early Childhood Education.* New York: Dial Press, 1973.

Kornhaber, A., and K. L. Woodward. *Grandparents and Grandchildren: The Vital Connection*. New York: Doubleday and Company, 1981.

Miller, B. L., and A. L. Wilmhurst. *Parents and Volunteers in the Classroom*. Palo Alto, CA: R and E Research Associates, 1975.

Morrison, G. S. *Parent Involvement in the Home, School, and Community*. Columbus, OH: Charles E. Merrill Publishing Company, 1978.

Newman, S. *Guidelines to Parent-Teacher Cooperation in Early Childhood Education*. Brooklyn, NY: Book-Lab, 1971.

Peterson, K. L., and J. E. Raven, "Guidelines for Supervising Student Teachers," *Child Care Information Exchange*, Sept./Oct. 1983, pp. 27–29.

Reagan, N. *To Love a Child*. New York: Bobbs-Merrill Company, Inc., 1982.

*School Volunteer Programs: Everything You Need to Know to Start or Improve your Program*. Alexandria, VA: National School Volunteer Program, Inc., 1981.

## CHAPTER 9 NOTES

1. E. H. Berger. *Parents as Partners in Education*. St. Louis, MO: C. V. Mosby Company, 1981, p. 93.

2. A. Kornhaber and K. L. Woodward. *Grandparents and Grandchildren: The Vital Connection*. New York: Doubleday and Company, 1981, p. 89.

3. Ibid., p. 97.

4. Ibid.

# CHAPTER 10

# Funding Sources and Other Techniques for Providing Staff Development

DURING THE first half of the 1970s, preschool programs enjoyed a heyday. Funds for day-care and preschool education were abundant. Staff could choose on-site training, conference attendance, college tuition reimbursement, and even consultant-specialist evaluation to further their professional development. The federal government and other sources were generous and involved. Training was available even on a large scale in some parts of the United States. Colleges, universities, school districts, and research groups received grants to enable them to develop and implement inservice programs.

By the late 1970s, however, the well began to run dry. Title XX of the Social Security Act, by far the largest source of federal support for day care, was replaced by the Social Service Block Grant. Based upon state population, an allocation is provided that must be divided up among a number of social services programs. The result has been a significant drop in the share of funds received by child-care programs. Although concern about child abuse in day care has resulted in recent additional allocations for day-care staff training to the Block Grant, funds for staff development are not considered abundant.

The turn away from federal involvement in day-care and preschool programs is not surprising in lieu of the trend toward overall government disinvestiture in social services, but it is disconcerting in light of demographic data that indicate that 46.7 million American women are employed outside the home.[1] Some sources predict that by the end of the century, 80 percent of American families with two parents will have two working parents.[2]

Without federal support and a national day-care policy, employers, community groups, churches, and private individuals have stepped in to create needed day-care slots. The cost of early childhood programs continues to mount, however, and with a strong lobby among professionals for better salaries for teachers and caregivers, little money is left over for staff development activities.

One of the challenges to early childhood leadership in the future is to discover alternatives that will address staff development needs. In this chapter we will discuss some of the options available to all of those administrators interested in finding innovative ways to promote professional development of staff.

## PURSUING FEDERAL FUNDING

It would be a serious error on the part of the authors of this book to suggest to readers that federal monies are no longer available for day-care and preschool programs. In fact, millions of dollars are made available annually to programs meeting the needs of young children and their families. These funds can be sought as one of the alternative ways to finance staff development. One of the differences in the way that funds are now distributed is that they are rarely allocated to fund entire programs. Rather, the monies may be granted in response to the need to develop a particular component of the program, pilot test an evaluative or developmental aspect of program, or may be provided as a match to existing funds.

The keys to access of federal dollars are two: (1) awareness of sources of monies and skills for developing the right proposal and (2) finding out which government agencies have funds, which is not difficult. The government prints several publications the purpose of which is to announce grant possibilities. A director can subscribe to these information sources or find issues in the local branch of the public library. Some of these government publications are:

1. *Catalog of Federal Domestic Assistance*—Published once each year, the catalog provides a comprehensive list of all federally funded programs. Each program is described according to its purpose, goals, rules of eligibility, and application procedures. The catalog can be ordered from the Superintendent of Documents, U.S. Government Printing Office, Washington, DC 20402.

2. *Federal Register*—This is a daily updating of proposed changes in the code of Federal Regulations. Information about the due dates for proposals for federal funding and the criteria by which applicants for funds are selected is also described. The Federal Register should not be relied upon as the only source of information about federal funds, but it can be very useful. It is available, by subscription, from the Government Printing Office or in the local public library.

3. *Commerce Business Daily*—This is another daily publication of the U.S. Government. It announces requests for proposals, proposal procurement, and contract awards. The focus of this publication is contracts rather than grant notices, and it would be useful to larger school systems or universities seeking government training or staff development contracts. *Commerce Business Daily* is available at the local public library or through the Government Printing Office.

4. *American Education/Guide to Office of Education Administered Programs—American Education*—This is published ten times annually in order to provide the public with an overview of the activities of the Department of Education. The *Guide,* published annually by the Department, describes types of financial assistance available to educational programs, the purpose of funds, the amount of funding available (annual appropriation in dollars), who is eligible to apply for funds, and where to apply. To obtain copies of these publications visit your local public library, or write to the Department of Education, Washington, DC 20202.

Once aware of the sources of available funds, a director must begin the process of developing a proposal for use of the monies. Most government agencies provide application kits that give essential information and contain the necessary forms. These must be carefully studied in order to determine exactly what the applicant requirements are. Failure to provide a single critical piece of information, answer a question, or to fill in a blank space on a questionnaire can result in rejection of the entire proposal.

Another change from the proposals requested in the 1960s and 1970s is one of length. It was not unusual in 1972, for example, for admissions to be fifty or more pages long. Today those who read and evaluate proposals prefer those that are brief and to the point. Many application kits stipulate the length of the admission and will not consider proposals that exceed this length.

While some variations in proposal requirements occur, most applications request the same types of information.

1. An ABSTRACT of the funding request is usually expected. The abstract is a brief statement naming the submitting institution, describing the goals of the proposed project, providing an overview of the activities planned, and summarizing the projected costs of the project.

2. A BACKGROUND STATEMENT is the second crucial component of a proposal. This section addresses the institution or agency's purpose, its goals, and its manner of functioning in the community. The agency's suitability as a recipient of funds should be established in this part of the proposal. Unique qualifications and skills of staff can also be described here.

3. The NEEDS STATEMENT describes the problem that the proposed project will address and the needs underlying it. If data are to be included regarding clients or, for example, the need of the community for an infant care program, it should be located in this part of the proposal.

4. In the fourth segment of the proposal, the GOALS and OBJECTIVES of the project are stated. These should be clear and not too numerous. It is also important that there is a direct parallel between the goals of the funding source and those of the proposed project.

5. PROGRAM ACTIVITIES are the fifth component of the proposal. This is the section that addresses the techniques that will be used to implement the project. If funds are requested for staff development, the training and education activities that will comprise the program are briefly detailed here.

6. PROGRAM EVALUATION describes the measures and techniques that will be used to determine what impact the project will have. The tools to be used to collect data, the frequency with which they will be used, and the means of analysis should be described. It should be pointed out that the degree of accountability established is an increasingly important factor in the selection of grantees.

7. The last of the frequently requested parts of proposals is the all essential BUDGET. The budget should contain the carefully estimated costs of salaries and fringe benefits, materials and equipment, consultants, tuitions, and other services utilized.

Taking care to meet all the required criteria and submit the proposal on time increases the chances that funding requests will be positively responded to. One last comment on proposal development. Some government agencies will provide feedback on proposals when funding requests are denied. Rather than viewing this as a criticism, these comments may be used to upgrade future efforts through proposal writing to finance staff development.

## FOUNDATION GRANTS

A number of philanthropic groups and charitable organizations, some founded by wealthy families, fund the projects of early childhood programs. The processes for identifying and appealing to foundations are not dissimilar to those associated with pursuit of federal funds. There are directories available that list private grantors, their headquarters, describe their primary interests and goals, and the amounts of money distributed annually. These volumes also let the reader know how frequently funding applications are evaluated.

The best source of the directories and other information on private funding is the regional office of the Foundation Center National Libraries in your state. The location of the nearest foundation center can be obtained by writing to:

|  |  |  |
|---|---|---|
| The Foundation Center<br>888 Seventh Avenue<br>New York, NY 10019 | or | The Foundation Center<br>1001 Connecticut Avenue, N.W.<br>Washington, DC 20035 |

Additional sources of information on foundation funding and proposal writing are available through the following sources:

Education Funding Research Council
75 National Press Building, N.W.
Washington, DC 20045

Education News Services Division
Capitol Publications, Inc.
Suite G-128
2430 Pennsylvania Avenue, N.W.
Washington, DC 20037

Human Resources Network
2010 Chancellor Street
Philadelphia, PA 19103

National Rural Center
1828 L Street, N.W.
Washington, DC 20036

Public Management Institute
333 Hayes Street
San Francisco, CA 94102

Responsive Procurement Exchange
1204 Half Street, S.W.
Washington, DC 20024

Taft Corporation
1000 Vermont Avenue, N.W.
Washington, DC 20005

The Grantsmanship Center
1015 West Olympic Boulevard
Los Angeles, CA 90015

## CENTER-BASED FUND-RAISING EFFORTS

Another of the means to acquiring funds for staff development involves enlisting the support of staff, parents, and board members. Although they are not usually the best way to raise large sums, they can, nonetheless, pay for short-term commitment services, trips for staff to national conferences, a staff member's workshop tuition, and other special training events. Small fund-raising projects can support memberships in professional organizations, subscriptions to journals and periodicals, and the purchase of textbooks for staff attending college or reference books to be kept at the center.

Some of the ways that small sums of money can be raised include:

- Bake sales—scheduled close to big holidays; buyers are interested in stocking up on goods for guests, large family dinners, and picnics

- Hoagie sales—scheduled a distance from holidays like Thanksgiving and Christmas, when buyers are concerned about dieting

- T-shirt sales—featuring the Center's name and logo can be a big seller among families, relatives, and friends of the center; effective during warm weather

- Raffles—featuring chances to win several attractive prizes in exchange for the purchase of an inexpensive ticket

- Flea markets—featuring goods and collectibles donated by the entire center family (parents, staff, board members)

- Car washes—run by staff and parents and following a stretch of rainy weather can bring in dollars for staff development

- Pot luck suppers—advertised locally and featuring platters of prepared food to be taken home by purchasers who sign up in advance of the event

- Candy sales—conducted with the aid of a reputable fund-raising candy company. Sales should be made by adults only, rather than children. Individual large chocolate bars and boxes of candy are often big sellers.

## ALTERNATIVE APPROACHES TO FUNDING PROGRAMS

The previous sections of this chapter have dealt with tools for funding more traditional staff development programs. Now some alternative approaches will be discussed, beginning with the concept of service-exchange programs.

### Service-Exchange Programs

Long before societies had systems of monetary exchange, people exchanged goods or services to obtain what was needed for survival. In recent years, many people have rediscovered the exchange system as a means for coping with a growing rate of inflation. In a similar fashion, systems of exchange, set up among professionals in the early childhood community, can be a virtually cost-free means to providing an effective staff development component. Figure 10–1 describes steps suggested for developing a service-exchange program. Some examples of service-exchange situations follow:

- A day-care center offers to be an observation site for students from a local college's child-development department. In return several faculty will conduct workshops for center staff.

- A director has recently completed training with a renowned infant specialist. She offers to make a presentation of what she has learned to staff from another program in return for their donation of used infant toys collected by that program's parents.

## STEPS FOR DEVELOPING A SERVICE EXCHANGE PROGRAM

I. Begin by mobilizing the local early childhood administrators group. If one does not exist, start one. Include representatives from local colleges and professional organizations.

II. Utilize a group meeting to present the service exchange concept and describe its benefits.

   A. Outline of the service-exchange program

   1. Each director surveys his or her staff development needs, and strengths and expertise.

   2. Directors present these in written form to the administrators' group at a later meeting.

   3. Directors list all of the skills and information they would be willing to share with other center staff. (A list of suggested exchanges could be provided to the group.)

   4. Directors may contract with one another to provide staff development activities or be the recipient of them.

   5. Directors will continually assess the value of the service-exchange program and suggest needed changes.

   B. Benefits of the service exchange program

   1. Staff in programs get to know one another, and networking is possible.

   2. Early childhood community is strengthened through enhanced sense of professionalism.

   3. Staff development goals are achieved without extra cost to programs.

   4. Individual programs may improve in quality.

   5. Staff development can be accomplished without necessarily removing staff from center or without staff shortages.

III. The administrators group should meet regularly to evaluate the service-exchange program, bringing with them staff input commands.

FIGURE 10–1

- Directors of two preschool programs agree to exchange teachers (one from each classroom) for a two-week period.

- A staff member from one center who is an expert carpenter agrees to build a special piece of climbing equipment for another center in return for lessons on cooking activities appropriate for young children from a teacher in the second center.

## Inservice Education Alternatives

The viability of directors as staff trainers has already been established in this book. If, however, an administrator is to achieve effective staff-development leadership, that individual must think and function in creative ways. If caregivers, teachers, and support staff are to be renewed by training activities, innovative ideas and techniques must be employed to stimulate interest and enhance learning opportunities.

There are numerous types of materials and techniques available to personnel trainers. Utilizing management training sources is one way to pinpoint the topics and educational devices that can be useful in many staff development activities. The local public library and regional management training centers operated by the U.S. government are two places that can be helpful in the search for training information. In addition, bookstores now carry many books related to management concerns. Many of the topics and techniques used in management training are useful across a broad spectrum of staff-development programs.

While it is not an original thought, one worthy of discussion involves a discovery made many years ago by business and industry. Having the knowledge and technical skills needed to accomplish tasks is but one of the factors affecting work performance. Management trainers also focus heavily on the personal and group dynamics elements of job satisfaction. Unfortunately, these are much neglected areas of staff development in early childhood settings. Teacher and caregiver training has focused mainly on aspects of curriculum development and implementation. Little or no time is devoted to the interpersonal skills and personal growth factors that are often instrumental in early childhood program success. Borrowed from management training, some of these important topics are:

- *Stress Management*—deals with the environmental, organizational, and personal factors that create stress in the work place; learning to manage personal time and developing strategies to lessen all stress-creating elements is emphasized; recognizing the high stress levels associated with human-service activities is crucial to staff well-being

- *Problem Solving*—explores group and individual processes for responding to problems; establishes a formula for attacking problems as they arise

- *Interpersonal Relationships*—focuses on recognition of and appropriate responses to individual differences in priorities, standards, and values; establishes how understanding these can create conflicts between people and how learning to accept and value differences in order to integrate everyone's abilities and talents is essential in the early childhood setting

- *Communication Skills*—examines the different ways that people communicate information to one another, including verbal, written, and nonverbal (facial expression and body language) forms; addresses the different types of language often used by caregivers and parents and the barriers that can result

One of the more popular tools utilized by management trainers is the "simulation game."[3] It employs a hypothetical situation or problem that must be resolved by the group. The result is that interpersonal, problem solving, communication and other skills may be developed. While not everyone is comfortable with the group games approach, it is, nonetheless, an effective approach to dealing with some of the training issues facing early childhood program directors.

## Community Resources for Training Early Childhood Educators

In the search for training topics and options, directors often become tired. They feel that they have exhausted their resources, human and financial, having tapped into all of the leaders in the child-development and early childhood professions. For this reason, we conclude this chapter with our encouragement to think of the community as a learning environment. The entire community is filled with individuals and events that can enhance the skills of caregivers and support staff. Health-care professionals involved in research and practice regularly have new information to share that makes an impact on child, family, and staff well-being. Craftspersons and artisans have experience with materials and techniques that can be used to enhance children's creativity and self-expression. Product manufacturers use materials that can facilitate sensory and cognitive growth. In short, no resource for knowledge or skills should be overlooked.

Lastly, the authors recommend developing a wellness program. Aimed at providing support systems for caregivers and other human service personnel, a wellness program offers a forum for discussion of problems and interests common to the group. It may also provide group outlets for various stresses experienced by individuals. Jogging, aerobics, bowling, and social outings are some of the stress reducers that may be employed by the group. Staff development is no longer a matter of learning new ways to facilitate children's learning. Today, just as the profession speaks of responding to the needs of the whole child, the authors urge a program of overall growth, professional and personal, for every member of the early childhood staff.

## RECOMMENDED READING

Allen, H. *The Bread Game: The Realities of Foundation Fund Raising*, Fourth Revised Edition. San Francisco: Regional Young Adult Project, 1981.

Ardman, P., and H. Ardman. *The Woman's Day Book of Fund Raising*. New York: St. Martins Press, 1981.

Dodge, A. B., and D. F. Tracy (eds.). *How to Raise Money for Kids (Public and Private)*. Washington, DC: Coalition for Children and Youth, 1978.

Finn, M. *Fund Raising for Early Childhood Programs: Getting Started and Getting Results*. Washington, DC: National Association for the Education of Young Children, 1982.

*Fund Raising* (Reprint No. 10). Redmond, WA: Child Care Information Exchange.

Mager, R. F. *Preparing Instructional Objectives*. Belmont, CA: Fearon Publishers, 1962.

Otterbourg, S. *School Partnerships Handbook: How to Set Up and Administer Programs with Business, Government, and Your Community*. Englewood Cliffs, NJ: Prentice-Hall, 1986.

Warren, P. B. *The Dynamics of Funding: An Educator's Guide to Effective Grantsmanship*. Boston: Allyn and Bacon, 1980.

## CHAPTER 10 NOTES

1. Select Committee on Children, Youth, and Families: Demographic and Social Trends, "Implications for Federal Support of Dependent Care Services for Children and the Elderly," U.S. Government Printing Office, Washington, DC, 1984.

2. D. Meredith. "Day Care: The Nine-to-Five Dilemma," *Psychology Today,* February 1986, p. 38.

3. R. E. Howe and A. Cleaves (eds.). *The Guide to Simulations/Games for Education and Training,* Fourth Edition. Beverly Hills, CA: Sage Publications, 1980.

# CHAPTER 11

## Evaluating Staff Development Programs

ONE OF THE most important aspects of staff-development programs is that of assessing their impact. Although there are a great many tools and processes for looking at the results of these activities, all serve one primary purpose, that is, to determine whether change has occurred due to specific parts of the staff-development program.

Evaluation can address many questions about an early childhood program's effectiveness. It is a way to determine the success of staff development efforts and to survey its outcomes. Ultimately, staff development should positively affect the total program for children and families. The modes of evaluation utilized can study questions of the early childhood program's ability to meet family and community needs; the appropriateness and effectiveness of policies and procedures; whether the program is being implemented as directed; and the benefits of the program to children and families (see Figure 11–1).

This chapter will focus on a discussion of the kinds, types, and measures of staff development assessment. The relationship and impact of staff development and training to the whole early childhood program will be presented.

## KINDS OF EVALUATION

Michael Scriven[1] has written about two general kinds of evaluation: formative and summative. Formative evaluation is a process approach that tends to be an ongoing system of data gathering designed to upgrade a program. This kind of evaluation is usually conducted by members of the program staff and may well be a built-in feature of the program. An example of formative evaluation in an early childhood program is a regular assessment of children's progress through observations and use of developmental rating scales.

The second kind of evaluation, according to Scriven, is summative.[2] Unlike the formative method, summative evaluation is focused upon the program's products. Summative evaluation occurs at a particular point in the school year and is designed to look at the overall success of the program. The goals and objectives for the program may be used as the criteria for measuring success. Summative evaluation is sometimes conducted by outside consultants, rather than by staff members. Examples of summative evaluation in early childhood include financial audits and end-of-the-year program reports.

Of the two kinds, this chapter will address the use of formative evaluation

## RELATIONSHIP OF STAFF TRAINING TO
## EARLY CHILDHOOD PROGRAM COMPONENTS

**Training Topic**

Environment

Choosing learning materials

Classroom arrangement

Outdoor learning space

Identifying traffic patterns

Repairing equipment

Creating interest centers

Scheduling free-choice activities

Field trips


Classroom management

Stress management

Time management

Interpersonal skills

Problem solving

Communications skills

Personal growth/self-actualization

Parent-child relationships

Home-school relationships


Creative expression

Units/themes for study

Developing lesson activity plans

Observing/recording children's behavior

Language arts

Pre-math concepts

Child development

Social studies concepts

Science skills

**Program Component to Be Evaluated**

Impacts on: Physical Setting

Impacts on: Interactional Setting

Impacts on: Children's Program

FIGURE 11–1

as that one most appropriate to examining the impact on staff development. The reasons for this choice are twofold:

1. If staff development efforts are ongoing, so should the evaluation process be. The messages that come from regular evaluation provide direction for additional activities and clear pictures about the overall program.

2. The second purpose for the use of formative evaluation stems from problems associated with summative kinds. When an evaluation is conducted and difficulties are found, it is a much simpler process to recognize them soon after their occurrence than to have problems looming large and distant from the point of origin. Summative evaluation often unearths inappropriate and ineffective aspects of a program long after they have had a significant impact on participants. If the primary goal of staff development is improving program quality, each activity along the way should be appraised to determine its contribution and value.

## TYPES OF EVALUATION

While the growth of skills and knowledge can be measured at the time of staff training, there are specific areas of an early childhood program that can be examined for changes resulting from staff development.

The effectiveness of management can be studied. Assuring that the program complies with state and local regulations, that staff carry out assigned responsibilities, and that there are appropriate administration-staff communications are some of the considerations in management evaluation.

Analyzing the functioning and impact of the early childhood program is another type of evaluation. Taking account of each of the program components, how they operate independently and as a unit, and whether purposes of the program are being met are some of the areas to be scrutinized.

Studies of cost effectiveness can also be pursued. It is important for administration to be aware of how appropriately funds to staff and to operate the program are being used. Of special concern in this instance are expenditures made for staff development activities. Knowing which of the training activities are producing results can prevent many unnecessary expenditures. Training can be responsible for caregivers making more resourceful use of materials and time to accomplish the goals of the program. Ultimately, this means financial savings for the program.

## COMPONENTS FOR EVALUATION

Evaluation should consider three primary components of an early childhood program: the physical setting, human interactions, and the children's program.

## The Physical Setting

The physical setting includes those concrete aspects of the environment as it makes an impact on the program. Materials and equipment and their arrangement, the use of space provided, room temperature, and lighting are all examples of factors in the physical settings.

## Human Interactions

The interactions of people in the early childhood center comprise a second program component. The language and communications skills used, as well as individual and group stress levels heavily affect the ways individuals relate to one another. Child-child, teacher-child, staff-staff, and parent-staff interactions should all be studied.

## The Children's Program

The children's program, a third component, consists of the curriculum developed, teaching strategies employed, the climate in which implementation occurs, and evaluation measures utilized. Refer back to Figure 11-1 for some examples of the relationship between staff development and components of programs for young children.

### MEASURES OF TRAINING SUCCESS

Having addressed evaluation of programs as one of the means to assess the consequences of staff development, this section of this chapter will be devoted to evaluation techniques that measure changes in the knowledge and abilities of staff. These methods and instruments are designed primarily for use soon after the completion of training. Some methods are designed for use by learners, others are to be used by administrators or parents. Each provides specific feedback on a training activity.

## Pre-Test/Post-Test Systems

One method of evaluation that utilizes specific criteria is the pre-test/post-test system. The pre-test is designed to look at the status of staff skills and information prior to a training activity. If it has already been established that training is needed in a particular topic area, the pre-test is likely to reveal clear-cut deficits. The training is designed to rectify these. At its conclusion, a similar test that surveys the same skills is administered. The outcome of post-tests provides information on training's aftereffects.

This system of evaluation can be presented in written form. However, when an attempt is being made to develop caregiver competencies through training, a combination of observation and written tests is probably appropriate. Observations that form an aspect of the pre-test/post-test system cannot be random. The behaviors and language desired should be accurately described prior to the observation. This is the type of criteria referred to in the observation form provided in Chapter 8.

A second critical factor in the establishment of test criteria is the predetermination of those factors that constitute test mastery. It may be that certain written or observed skills must be appropriately demonstrated before a staff member is considered to have "passed" the test. Another way of handling the scoring question is to require caregivers to earn a particular number of points in order to achieve mastery.

One caution about all testing systems involves the very human tendency to compare grades received. Staff training should not be an activity that stimulates unhealthy competition. Test should also be as free of racial and cultural biases as possible.

## Control-Group Measures

When a large staff is involved, some directors may find that the use of a control group to evaluate training is both economical and informative. This type of measurement requires the comparison of two caregiver groups, one that receives training (experimental) and one that does not (control). If the skills deficits of staff have previously been identified, an evaluator can compare the competencies of both groups of caregivers following training. The degree of difference between the control and experimental groups, after accounting for any variables that could affect the results, determines the impact of training activities. If there is significant improvement in the competence of the experimental group and no other variables (such as conference or college course attendance) are present to account for changes, then this growth can be attributed to training.

It should be noted that while knowledge of statistics is helpful when control-group measures are used, it is not essential. Results can be analyzed in simple percentage terms. This type of measurement would be a cost-effective means of looking at a potential training program prior to making a commitment to it. Large school systems with child-care programs and day-care centers employing large numbers of staff might consider control-group measures of evaluation.

## Evaluations Based upon Parental Input

A far less exacting means of evaluating training involves soliciting parents' input about staff competence. While it is not recommended as the only means for assessing training outcomes, rating scales or other evaluations completed by parents can have a very positive impact on the overall program and can convey information about the growth of caregivers' skills. When used, evaluations should be conducted in a discrete, confidential manner to avoid any damage to parent-staff relationships.

Requesting parents' feedback about staff has several potential results. It should be done with staffs' knowledge; therefore, the parent's role as client and consumer of services is reinforced. The individual parent is empowered by this request. The right to acknowledge parental concerns and the strengths and weaknesses of the program is validated.

As with the Child Development Associate Credential Award System, it is possible to request that parents evaluate a single caregiver or classroom environment at a time. This should always be conducted discretely, using a written format. Information received by the evaluator is treated confidentially, with the summarized results released only to the staff and parents. In some programs individual evaluations by parents may not be appropriate. Each director must decide which is most suitable for parents' assessment, the individual or group evaluation (see Figure 11–2).

## Staff Self-Evaluation

In many ways it is fitting to close this book with mention of the importance of self-evaluation. It is one of the skills that the authors most value and consider essential for educators at all levels. It is what teacher training institutions neglect to teach. It can sustain a teacher at difficult times, turning mistakes into challenges to be overcome.

No staff development activity should ever be undertaken or completed without learners' input. That input should not merely be requested for the benefit of the trainer or program administrator. If training is to be truly successful, the individual staff member must also be aware of the initial deficits and, later, the growth accomplished.

It is difficult, if not impossible, to teach someone to self-evaluate because the process is different for everyone. A trainer can, however, suggest the areas that staff members might review in considering their professional development. Since the type of self-evaluation suggested here is that which looks only at learners' interpretations of how they have been affected by training, a session might conclude with caregivers and trainer brainstorming to identify self-evaluation criteria (see Figure 11–3).

Self-evaluation can also be facilitated if a format is provided for staff. One that is very useful to persons unfamiliar with the self-evaluation process involves the partnership model. Each participant in training is asked to select a partner. Given general criteria selected by the group, each set of partners is asked to observe and provide feedback as objectively as possible on one another's performance. Then, each trainee responds in writing to this critique,

## PARENTS' STAFF EVALUATION FORM FOLLOWING
## CLASSROOM MANAGEMENT TRAINING (GROUP EVALUATION)

Dear Parents:

Members of the staff of the Grant Child Development Center have recently completed an inservice program designed to improve skills for working with the children. Your perception of how teachers interact with children would be very helpful to us at this time. Please indicate your answers to the following statements, and return this questionnaire to your child's teacher. Thank you for your cooperation and assistance. Your honest answers to these questions will help us to have a better program. Feel free sign your name, or you may remain anonymous if you wish.

Yvette Monroe,
Director

(Check One)

| | Often | Sometimes | Rarely |
|---|---|---|---|
| 1. Children in the classroom seem busy and happy. | _____ | _____ | _____ |
| 2. Children in the classroom fight with one another. | _____ | _____ | _____ |
| 3. Teachers tell children the rules of the classroom. | _____ | _____ | _____ |
| 4. Children seem to know what is expected of them. | _____ | _____ | _____ |
| 5. Teachers use quiet, firm voices when talking to the children. | _____ | _____ | _____ |
| 6. Teachers have to scold and correct children for misbehavior. | _____ | _____ | _____ |
| 7. Teachers are cooperative and friendly in their work and their interactions with one another. | _____ | _____ | _____ |
| 8. Teachers listen when children talk to them. | _____ | _____ | _____ |
| 9. Children respond when teachers talk to them. | _____ | _____ | _____ |
| 10. It is very noisy in the classroom. | _____ | _____ | _____ |

**FIGURE 11–2**